STRATEGIC STUDIES INSTITUTE

The Strategic Studies Institute (SSI) is part of the U.S. Army War College and is the strategic-level study agent for issues related to national security and military strategy with emphasis on geostrategic analysis.

The mission of SSI is to use independent analysis to conduct strategic studies that develop policy recommendations on:

- Strategy, planning, and policy for joint and combined employment of military forces;

- Regional strategic appraisals;

- The nature of land warfare;

- Matters affecting the Army's future;

- The concepts, philosophy, and theory of strategy; and,

- Other issues of importance to the leadership of the Army.

Studies produced by civilian and military analysts concern topics having strategic implications for the Army, the Department of Defense, and the larger national security community.

In addition to its studies, SSI publishes special reports on topics of special or immediate interest. These include edited proceedings of conferences and topically oriented roundtables, expanded trip reports, and quick-reaction responses to senior Army leaders.

The Institute provides a valuable analytical capability within the Army to address strategic and other issues in support of Army participation in national security policy formulation.

i

Strategic Studies Institute
and
U.S. Army War College Press

TRIBAL MILITIAS:
AN EFFECTIVE TOOL TO COUNTER AL-QAIDA AND ITS AFFILIATES?

Norman Cigar

November 2014

*****

Comments pertaining to this report are invited and should be forwarded to: Director, Strategic Studies Institute and U.S. Army War College Press, U.S. Army War College, 47 Ashburn Drive, Carlisle, PA 17013-5010.

*****

This manuscript was funded by the U.S. Army War College External Research Associates Program. Information on this program is available on our website, *www.StrategicStudies Institute.army.mil*, at the Opportunities tab.

*****

The Strategic Studies Institute and U.S. Army War College Press publishes a monthly email newsletter to update the national security community on the research of our analysts, recent and forthcoming publications, and upcoming conferences sponsored by the Institute. Each newsletter also provides a strategic commentary by one of our research analysts. If you are interested in receiving this newsletter, please subscribe on the SSI website at *www.StrategicStudiesInstitute.army.mil/newsletter*.

*****

I would like to express my gratitude to Dr. Christopher Harmon for his valuable insights and suggestions on the initial proposal for this study.

FOREWORD

Most of the local societies in which Al-Qaida and its affiliates and offshoots operate in the Middle East and Africa have a predominantly tribal or at least have a strong tribal component (Iraq, Yemen, Libya, Syria, Somalia, Mali, and Sinai). Countering Al-Qaida's continuing presence, therefore, requires addressing the tribal milieu and understanding Al-Qaida's critical vulnerabilities when it operates in tribal societies. In this context, the capability that tribally-based militias provide may be one of the most effective tools against Al-Qaida, and may offer a cost-effective mechanism serving as a force multiplier for U.S. forces. It could reduce the need for U.S. force commitment on the ground in environments that might offer unfavorable conditions for a U.S. Landpower footprint.

It is important to appreciate the vulnerabilities that Al-Qaida faces in dealing with tribes inherent in the dilemma between implementing its ideological and political program and the social realities that are likely to generate conflict, such as Islamic vs. tribal law, folk religion, social and economic mores, and the presence of outsiders, not including the challenge to traditional tribal leaderships that Al-Qaida's influence may entail. Given this environment, it is therefore not surprising that tribally-based militias can be organized and function as an effective supportive counter in the effort against Al-Qaida.

In this monograph, Dr. Norman Cigar identifies two models for tribal militias—either managed by local governments and supported by outside patrons or managed directly by an outside agent. The resulting dynamic is most often a triangular one among Al-Qaida, the tribes, and the local government. It must be studied within that perspective, as Al-Qaida "has a vote" in the ensuing struggle as it attempts to adapt.

Dr. Cigar focuses on the experience in Iraq and Yemen, but some lessons learned may be applicable more broadly. While the positive results may be significant, as in the case of Iraq and Yemen, there are cautionary guidelines to be drawn from past experience for the creation and functioning of such tribal militias that could mark the difference between success or ultimate failure, including balancing the local government's dilemma between encouraging an effective counter to Al-Qaida and managing the threat from such autonomous forces in the long run.

This monograph notes a number of lessons learned for the United States while acting as the direct managing patron of these groups. Among them are the following:

- to understand the strengths and limitations of tribal militias and shape the latter's roles and missions accordingly;
- to support a tribal militia adequately in material terms;
- to provide effective protection for key tribal militia leaders;
- to ensure that the U.S. management and use of tribal militias do not undercut an existing or emerging government's legitimacy;
- to craft a realistic and effective demobilization plan; and to conduct an effective information campaign directed toward the parent tribes.

When the United States acts as a support agent for tribal militias managed by a local government, the lessons learned include:

- providing funding, arms, selected operational support, and intelligence;
- advising the local government on how to best deal with the tribal militias; and,
- advising and supporting other countries that might act in the future as potential patrons of tribal militias.

The Strategic Studies Institute is pleased to offer this monograph as part of its continuing effort to inform the debate on dealing with the continuing threat of Al-Qaida and related movements. This analysis should be useful to help strategic leaders, planners, intelligence professionals, and commanders to better understand the challenges of the contemporary strategic landscape in the Middle East and to craft effective responses.

DOUGLAS C. LOVELACE, JR.
Director
Strategic Studies Institute and
  U.S. Army War College Press

ABOUT THE AUTHOR

NORMAN CIGAR is a Research Fellow at the Marine Corps University, Quantico, VA, from which he retired recently as Director of Regional Studies and the Minerva Research Chair. Previously, he had also taught at the Marine Corps Command and Staff College and at the Marine Corps School of Advanced Warfighting. In an earlier assignment, he spent 7 years as a senior political-military analyst in the Pentagon, Washington, DC, where he was responsible for the Middle East in the Office of the Army's Deputy Chief of Staff for Intelligence, and supported the Secretary of the Army, the Chief of Staff of the Army, and Congress with intelligence. He also represented the Army on national-level intelligence issues in the interagency intelligence community. During the Gulf War, he was the Army's senior political-military intelligence staff officer on the Desert Shield/Desert Storm Task Force. He has also taught at the National Intelligence University and was a Visiting Fellow at the Institute for Conflict Analysis & Resolution, George Mason University. He has studied and traveled widely in the Middle East. Dr. Cigar is the author of numerous works on politics and security issues dealing with the Middle East and the Balkans, and has been a consultant at the International Criminal Tribunal for the former Yugoslavia at the Hague. Among his writings are *Al-Qa'ida's Doctrine for Insurgency*; *Al-Qaida, the Tribes, and the Government; Lessons and Prospects for Iraq's Unstable Triangle*; and the forthcoming *Al-Qaida and the Arab Spring: Reacting to Surprise and Adapting to Change*. Dr. Cigar holds a DPhil from Oxford (St Antony's College) in Middle East history and Arabic; an M.I.A. from the School of International and Public Affairs and a Certificate from the Middle East Institute, Columbia University; and an M.S.S.I. from the National Intelligence University.

SUMMARY

Despite over a decade of open war, dealing with Al-Qaida and its affiliates in the Middle East is likely to remain a concern for the foreseeable future and will pose a challenge requiring the use of any tool that is likely to be effective in meeting the threat. Most of the local societies in which Al-Qaida has operated in the Middle East and Africa after September 11, 2001, have a predominantly tribal character or at least have a strong tribal component (Iraq, Yemen, Libya, Syria, Somalia, Mali, and Sinai). Developing effective tools to counter Al-Qaida's continuing presence in that social environment, therefore, is a priority and requires understanding Al-Qaida's critical vulnerabilities when it operates in those societies and developing the means to counter Al-Qaida's efforts.

This monograph addresses the role of tribal militias in the context of the fight against Al-Qaida. The intent is to enrich policy analysis and clarify options for future operations by focusing on past experience in order to identify the positive and negative aspects related to the use of such militias. The focus in this monograph is on Iraq and Yemen. However, many of the lessons learned may be applied more broadly. The thesis is that the capabilities which tribally-based militias provide may be one of the most efficient, cost-effective tools against Al-Qaida. In some cases, such militias can act as a force multiplier for U.S. Landpower forces, whether deployed on the ground in significant numbers, or, in other cases, if such militias can reduce the need for a U.S. commitment on the ground in environments that might present unfavorable conditions for a significant U.S. Landpower footprint. At the same time, given the complexity of the local political environment, tribal militias are no panacea, but can be a two-edged sword. Like any weapon, the use of tribal militias has to be understood and wielded with caution and skill in order to avoid unintended consequences.

This discussion includes two models for the tribal militias based on the nature of their patron. In Model 1, the patron of a militia is an outside entity; in Model 2, the national government is the patron (although an outside entity may provide ancillary support). The first case study deals with a Model 1 situation, where a foreign patron — the United States — acted in that role in Iraq beginning in late-2006 and lasting through the hand-over to Iraqi authorities during the period from December 2008 to April 2009. The second case study deals with two ongoing Model 2 situations, again with Iraq, but taking place after the national government's assumption of responsibility for the tribal militia in 2009. This case study is especially useful for comparative purposes with the first case study. The third case study deals with Yemen, where the local government has acted as the militia patron since 2012.

Based on the experience from Iraq and Yemen, this monograph concludes that the positive results of using tribal militias in the fight against Al-Qaida and its offshoots may be significant. Within the context of fighting against Al-Qaida, encouraging and supporting any armed local constituency — such as Iraq's tribes — may be a reasonable or even an unavoidable option at a particular juncture in time for an outside power or for a local patron in dealing with that insurgency. Nevertheless, as is often true in the real world, this is not a panacea and, based on past experience, there are cautionary guidelines to be remembered for the creation and functioning of such tribal militias that could make the difference between success or ultimate failure. Each of the two models studied has political and military advantages and disadvantages, but one may not have the luxury of which option to select in a specific situation.

Among the recommendations for policy in those situations where the United States is a tribal militia's direct patron are to:

- understand the strengths and limitations of tribal militias and shape the latter's roles and missions accordingly;
- support a tribal militia adequately in material terms;
- provide effective protection for key tribal militia leaders from inevitable Al-Qaida efforts to eliminate them;
- ensure that the U.S. management and use of tribal militias do not undercut an existing or emerging government's legitimacy;
- craft a realistic and effective demobilization plan; and,
- conduct an effective information campaign directed toward the tribes.

When the United States is in a supporting role to the local government, among the recommendations are to:

- provide funding, arms, selected operational support, and intelligence channeled through the patron local government;
- advise the local government as to the best way to deal with the tribal militias; and,
- advise and support other countries that might act in the future as potential patrons of tribal militias.

TRIBAL MILITIAS:
AN EFFECTIVE TOOL TO COUNTER AL-QAIDA AND ITS AFFILIATES?

INTRODUCTION

Despite over a decade of open war, dealing with Al-Qaida in the Middle East is likely to remain a concern for the foreseeable future and will pose a challenge requiring the use of any tool that is likely to be effective in meeting the threat. Most of the local societies in which Al-Qaida and its affiliates have operated in the Middle East and Africa after September 11, 2001, have a predominantly tribal character or at least have a strong tribal component (Iraq, Yemen, Libya, Syria, Somalia, Mali, and Sinai). Developing effective tools to counter Al-Qaida's continuing presence in that social environment, therefore, is a priority and requires understanding Al-Qaida's critical vulnerabilities when it operates in those societies and developing the means to counter Al-Qaida's efforts.

In particular, this monograph addresses the role of tribal militias in the context of the fight against Al-Qaida. The intent is to enrich policy analysis and clarify options for future operations by focusing on past experience in order to identify the positive and negative aspects related to the use of such militias.

The thesis is that the capabilities which tribally-based militias provide may be one of the most efficient and cost-effective tools against Al-Qaida. In some cases, such militias can act as a force multiplier for U.S. Landpower forces, whether deployed on the ground in significant numbers, or, in other cases, if such militias can reduce the size or preclude the need for a U.S. commitment on the ground in environments that might present unfavorable conditions for a significant U.S. Landpower footprint. At the same time, given the complexity of the local political environment, tribal militias are no panacea, but can be a two-edged sword and, like any weapon, this weapon has to be understood and wielded with caution and skill in order to avoid unintended consequences.

Terms of Reference and Methodology.

This monograph examines two models for tribal militias, categorized on the basis of the nature of their patron, since this is a key factor insofar as affecting a patron's interests, the patron-tribe relationship, Al-Qaida's strategy, and the short- and long-term structure and the political and military functioning of tribal militias. In Model 1, the patron of a militia is an outside entity; in Model 2, the national government is the patron (although an outside patron may provide ancillary support). The intent of the analysis is to extract lessons learned from which to craft recommendations for the future that can facilitate the development of effective policies and techniques by U.S. policymakers for optimal use of assets in dealing with Al-Qaida. Of course, every country in the Middle East has a unique history and society, with a specific tribal social structure and role in the national political system, as well as being subject to differences in the local geostrategic environment. The focus here is on Iraq and Yemen. However, many of the lessons learned may be applicable more broadly. Likewise, although the analysis relies on data up to mid-2014 and future developments cannot be foreseen in detail, nevertheless these general lessons learned should remain valid.

The focus is on dealing with insurgent groups inspired by Al-Qaida, even if they are not always controlled by the traditional Al-Qaida leadership. In that context, a clarification may be in order for the terms identifying these organizations as used here. In Iraq, the main jihadist organization has been through a number of name changes since its appearance in that country under the leadership of Abu Musab Al-Zarqawi in 2003 as the Monotheism and Jihad Group (*Jamaat Al-Tawhid wa'l-Jihad*). The group was renamed Al-Qaida in Mesopotamia (*Al-Qaida fi Bilad Al-Rafidayn*) in 2004 when Al-Zarqawi adhered formally to Usama Bin Ladin as leader of Al-Qaida. In October 2006, the Islamic State of Iraq (*Dawlat Al-Iraq Al-Islamiya*, or ISI) was proclaimed, although still maintaining at least nominal loyalty to Al-Qaida's central leadership.

In the wake of the Arab Spring, it was ISI that operated with delegated authority from Al-Qaida Central (by that time led by Ayman Al-Zawahiri), in Syria beginning in January 2012 through its creation, Jabhat Al-Nusra. However, the announcement by Abu Bakr Al-Husayni Al-Qurayshi Al-Baghdadi, head of ISI, on April 9, 2013, to the effect that he was establishing a joint Islamic State in Iraq and Syria (*Al-Dawla Al-Islamiya fi Al-Iraq wa'l-Sham* or ISIS), revealed openly the sharp differences over command relationships between the two adjoining theaters and with Al-Qaida Central's leadership.[1] Rejecting this initiative, Al-Zawahiri disowned the ISIS. With the beginning of Ramadan at the very end of June 2014, ISIS changed its name once again when it proclaimed itself the Islamic State (*Al-Dawla Al-Islamiya*), calling itself the Rightly-Guided Caliphate (*Al-Khilafa Al-Rashida*). Nevertheless, despite Al-Zawahiri's repudiation, Al-Baghdadi has continued to lay claim to Bin Ladin's mantle of leadership, and it may be a moot point as to which of the two—Al-Zawahiri or Al-Baghdadi's organization—now represents the Al-Qaida legacy.

Clearly, thanks to its success on the ground, ISIS has gained momentum and widespread recognition within Al-Qaida jihadist circles, and many prominent Al-Qaida figures now support it over a more isolated and contained Al-Zawahiri. Moreover, apart from Jabhat Al-Nusra's own website, only one of the traditional Al-Qaida websites—a key element in Al-Qaida's political outreach, legitimacy, and command and control system—still sides with Al-Zawahiri, as all the others by mid-2014 recognized and supported ISIS or, at best, remained silent on the split. In that sense, ISIS is still "Al-Qaida," whether Al-Zawahiri recognizes it as such or not. In this study, depending on the time period in question, the terms Al-Qaida/ISI are used when dealing with the earlier phase and ISIS when dealing with the more recent phase, although for practical purposes, the discussion is applicable to the broader Al-Qaida phenomenon.

In Yemen, the organization Al-Qaida in the Arabian Peninsula (*Al-Qaida fi Al-Jazira Al-Arabiya*) had resulted from the 2009 merger of Al-Qaida's branches in Saudi Arabia and Yemen. Under that name, Al-Qaida had already been battling against the Yemeni Army for several years by the time the Arab Spring broke out in Sanaa in early-2011. As was the case elsewhere in the Arab World, a new organization—the Supporters of the Law (*Ansar Al-Sharia*)—also appeared in Yemen although, even more clearly than elsewhere, there was in practice little substantive change, as the Ansar Al-Sharia were essentially part of Al-Qaida using a new name. In fact, very often it was impossible even for the Yemenis to differentiate between the two

4

names. In this monograph, the generic name Al-Qaida will be used for the organization in Yemen.

Three case studies will serve as the database and provide the context needed to understand the role of the tribal militias and the other players. The first case study deals with a Model 1 situation, where a foreign patron—the United States—acted in that role in Iraq from late-2006 through the December 2008-April 2009 period when responsibility was handed over to the Iraqi authorities. The second case study deals with a two Model 2 situation, again with Iraq, but in a Phase II, after the national government's assumption of responsibility for the tribal militia in 2009. This case study is especially useful for comparison with the earlier phase. The third case study deals with Yemen, where the local government has acted as the militia patron since 2012. Of course, the Yemeni and the Iraqi situations are ongoing, with the potential for evolution, but the general lines of development as identified here should provide sufficient information for an appreciation of the militia experience.[2]

Iraq and Yemen are both tribal societies, although in different ways. Since the "retribalization" of society for political reasons under Saddam Hussein in the 1990s, tribes have become an increasingly significant factor in Iraqi society, and even 80 percent of the urban population now is said to have a tribal allegiance.[3] In Yemen, tribes are perhaps the dominant political players in the country, and one can view even the Yemeni government itself as tribally-based to a significant extent, relying on certain "in-tribes," which is reflected in the composition of the military, police, bureaucracy, and funding for specific tribal regions. Iraqi tribal society is further complicated by sectarian and ethnic divisions between Sunni and Shia Arabs and

Sunni and Shia Kurds. Yemeni tribes, too, are divided between Sunni and various branches of the Shia.

Not surprisingly, the militias raised in both Iraq and Yemen to counter Al-Qaida have been essentially tribally-based both in terms of organization and personnel. To be sure, at times their name may not designate them as being "tribal," with the substitution of a euphemism intended to suggest a more modern organization rather than one based on a tribe, since a tribal label may carry a stigma in international circles or among local intellectuals. In Iraq, officially such militias have been known as the "Awakening" (*Sahwa*, or the plural *Sahwat*) — as well as Sons of Iraq and other names. However, the Iraqi media, in a nod to reality, at times also uses the term "Tribal Sahwa" (*Al-Sahwa Al-Asha'iriya*). In Yemen, the militias are most often known as "Popular Committees" (*Al-Lijan Al-Shabiya*) but here, again, the local media and participants are not shy about using the term "Tribal Committees" (*Al-Lijan Al-Qabaliya*).

Tribal militias do not exist in a vacuum: a country's tribal fabric, the character of a government, and Al-Qaida's overall relationship with the tribes provide the necessary background for understanding the tribal militias' functioning. In fact, the local government (or a foreign patron), the tribes, and Al-Qaida are all active players with their own interests, objectives, and strategies, and are forces that interact and seek to manipulate the other actors, thus forming an unstable triangular relationship. In this respect, it is particularly important to appreciate the vulnerabilities that Al-Qaida faces in dealing with tribes in general, vulnerabilities that are an inherent dilemma for Al-Qaida, as the latter is often caught between implementing its ideological and political program and dealing with social realities — and is a situation that is likely to generate conflict, as will be seen in the succeeding case studies.

MODEL 1

The Iraqi Experience — Phase I.

The tribal militias which emerged in Iraq in 2006 illustrate the Model 1 version of tribal militias, with a foreign entity, the United States, as the patron.

Developing the Sahwa.

Overall, the establishment and development of the Sahwa tribal militias can be seen as the result of a concurrence of interests in 2006 between a significant number of Sunni tribes and a foreign patron, the United States, which one could consider at the time the effective governing authority in the field in many areas of Iraq. With an active insurgency putting Al-Qaida and a spectrum of other smaller groups against the U.S. presence, the security situation — particularly in the country's Sunni areas — had reached a worrisome level that many found intractable. In order to engage in the jihad, Al-Qaida/ISI, of necessity, had to operate in the Sunni tribal milieu, which offered the most likely potential foundation for its effort. At first, Al-Qaida was able to make rapid inroads in the tribal community in Iraq, feeding on resentment against what was often viewed as an anti-Sunni and pro-Shia U.S. occupation. It was not alone in that, as other anti-U.S. militant groups representing disfranchised tribal elements, often linked to the proscribed Bath Party or the dissolved Iraqi military, also contributed to the insurgency.

Arguably, at the same time, Al-Qaida created its own unique critical vulnerabilities in Iraq by alienating the tribes and making them amenable to cooperating with U.S. forces. While, to some extent, aspects of Al-Qaida's policy were attributable to its ideological underpinnings of the organization as a whole, a more important factor was how the branch operating in Iraq chose to implement such principles in a range of practical situations.

Under its then-leader Abu Musab Al-Zarqawi, the local Al-Qaida clashed increasingly with tribal society by seeking to impose a strict interpretation of Sharia, or religious law, bolstered by religious courts handing down harsh sentences, in place of the traditional, more flexible, tribal law. Among the consequences of the enforcement of the Sharia were personal controls, such as banning music, shaving, and smoking, and restricting the role of women in public, as well as suppressing well-established elements of folk religion—such as invoking the intercession of saints or celebrating Muhammad's birthday (the *mulid*)—and interfering with marriage traditions. The high visibility of foreigners among Al-Qaida's leadership in Iraq, and the shunting aside of local clerics, only served as an additional irritant among the tribesmen, who are traditionally suspicious of outsiders. The violation of such tribal cultural values was felt as an unpardonable humiliation and, as one prominent shaykh, or tribal chief, put it, Al-Qaida's intent was to trample on the tribes' cherished values, that is to "do away with social custom (*urf ijtimai*) . . . that was the real goal of cutting off heads."[4]

Al-Qaida also insisted on a monopoly of control in the insurgency, either edging out or attacking competing armed groups, as well as being in the habit of launching indiscriminate attacks that often resulted in numerous civilian casualties. And, Al-Qaida was uncompromising: tribes had to choose sides — either with Al-Qaida or with the United States. Recalcitrant shaykhs were often assassinated.

However, it may have been, in particular, Al-Qaida's negative impact on the tribes' economic interests was decisive in estranging both the tribal leadership and ordinary tribesmen. Al-Qaida's violence in Al-Anbar and its growing control over the local society crippled the local economy and made U.S. projects unlikely given the lack of security, thereby undercutting the tribal shaykhs' influence as they could no longer broker economic benefits for their tribes. Al-Qaida also competed at times for control over the lucrative trade roads, a traditional source of some tribes' income. In the key case of Shaykh Abd Al-Sattar Abu Risha, who eventually became the most prominent U.S. ally in Al-Anbar province, a struggle with Al-Qaida for control of the main supply route from Amman to Baghdad pitted Al-Qaida against his tribe. Traditionally, Abu Risha's tribe had supplied most of region's truck drivers and may well have raided traffic and extorted tolls. During this struggle with Al-Qaida, prominent members of his family were killed.[5] It was this turn of events that induced Abd Al-Sattar to return from Jordan in 2006 and to approach the United States to join the fight against Al-Qaida.

Nevertheless, alone, the tribes — or the insurgent groups that were often intertwined with the tribes — realistically had been no match for Al-Qaida's organization, zeal, and ability to mass mobile forces from multiple locations against isolated tribes. Many tribes were reluctant to confront Al-Qaida, even as increasing numbers of their fellow-tribesmen joined the latter, because of its supposed dominance. Only gradually did the escalating disenchantment among tribesmen, accompanied by the increasing realization that co-operation might be possible with U.S. forces, change the environment.

U.S. policy had also evolved. At first, the United States was indifferent or hostile to the Sunni tribes. Because they were often tied to Saddam's power structure and were seen as part of a negative past, American leaders were reluctant to take advantage of a hospitable tribal terrain. Initially, as a former U.S. military intelligence officer noted to a reporter:

> [W]e couldn't get the CPA [Coalition Provisional Authority] to move . . . The standard answer we got from [CPA Head L. Paul] Bremer's people was that the tribes were a vestige of the past, that they have no place in the new democratic Iraq.[6]

By late-2005, U.S. forces on the ground were becoming more supportive of those tribes already in conflict with Al-Qaida. At that time, elements of what later coalesced into a general U.S. policy had already proved successful when they were attempted on a localized scale. For example, in 2005, one Army officer made an agreement with a local shaykh in return for construction projects and within a few weeks, "What had once been the most dangerous area in my zone became one of the safest."[7]

However, a strategic policy change from the American side emerged only in late-2006. At that time the unfavorable facts on the ground catalyzed a U.S. policy review leading to a revision in the counterinsurgency approach.[8] The key element of this revised approach was a greater willingness to partner with the Sunni tribes. These partnerships began initially in Al-Anbar and subsequently also in other Sunni areas, leading to the formation of a formal alliance in September 2006 between U.S. forces and a newly-established tribal organization—the Sahwa.

The Patron-Client Relationship.

To make the Sahwa a reality, the United States provided a range of tangible rewards that benefited both the shaykhs and ordinary tribesmen. These rewards included clothing, food, and public services. What was perhaps key were contracts to build or refurbish military facilities, pumping stations, roads, schools, clinics, and utility services, thanks to which, as one shaykh noted, "We were able to put our people to work."[9] Salaries for tribesmen serving in the Sahwa were an especially important inducement. According to one prominent shaykh, in just one section of Baghdad, the United States was supposedly paying $52 million a month on salaries to the Sahwa.[10] Equally important was the generous U.S. military assistance to the Sahwa—as well as to the local police—in the form of arms, ammunition, body armor, fuel, equipment, training, vehicles, and salaries for cooperating shaykhs, allowing the latter to field an organized, more or less full-time, military force under their control.[11] The shaykhs could now claim credit for having lifted the burden of Al-Qaida's oppressive presence from their fellow-tribesmen. At the same time, thanks to the relationship with the United States, shaykhs could strengthen their control over subordinates and clients in their tribes through the power of patronage and prestige. In fact, the United States, as a matter of policy, would seek to strengthen the power of cooperative shaykhs by providing contracts to the latter or, as one senior U.S. military officer was to note:

All of it [i.e., money] we funneled through the sheikhs.
. . . We empowered the sheikhs because there really
wasn't a government functioning. . . . And we did all
we could to empower the sheikhs.[12]

Especially crucial as an enabling factor was the
personal security that U.S. forces now provided to
important individual shaykhs, which addressed a
key vulnerability that Al-Qaida had been able to target up to then. Earlier, by simply eliminating selected
shaykhs, Al-Qaida had been generally successful in
nipping tribal resistance movements in the bud. Now,
on the contrary, U.S. forces, for example, even sat outside the Abu Risha compound and residence for almost a year.[13] While not fool-proof, the new personal
security regime afforded sufficient protection to convince shaykhs they could challenge Al-Qaida.

For the tribal shaykhs, the United States was the
ideal government, as it was a governing authority whose interest was primarily in security (and one
could argue that even the promotion of development
and providing services were tied to that primal interest) and which had little interest in interfering in
tribal affairs or in asking too many questions about a
shaykh's economic dealings. There was limited over-
sight into how the shaykhs spent the money which
flowed from the United States. As a senior U.S. military officer operating in Al-Anbar noted:

[T]here's a risk, because you're going to give him
[i.e., a shaykh] money, and you're not sure where the
money's going to go, because it's difficult for you to
get into that area, because of security, to ensure the
projects are being taken care of.[14]

Tribal forces joined the Sahwa in large numbers, and initiatives followed to replicate the Al-Anbar experience elsewhere. In some provinces, the Sahwa was set up considerably later, as in the case of Diyala, where it took until October 2008 to do so formally. Nevertheless, already by March 2008, the Sahwa nationwide numbered 91,000 personnel.

The Renewed War against Al-Qaida.

The establishment of the Sahwa—as the embodiment of the changed relationship with the tribes—was a key element in the turnaround of the situation with Al-Qaida, as it generated the large standing forces familiar with the local situation that could challenge Al-Qaida, at least with U.S. combat support. Conversely, recruiting the Sahwa also removed a significant portion of the active or potential personnel pool involved in the insurgency when they switched sides. In particular, the switching of allegiance by a shaykh could have significant influence on the security of an area. As Army Colonel Sean MacFarland noted of the situation in Al-Anbar, "Once a tribal leader flips, attacks on American forces in that area stop almost overnight."[15]

Of course, fielded U.S. military forces were also crucial to operational success against Al-Qaida, providing vital capabilities that the Sahwa could not. As a necessary complementary effort, U.S. forces (and Iraqi forces under U.S. guidance) could, and did, engage Al-Qaida in significant conventional operations, while also providing air and ground-based fires, force protection, intelligence, planning, logistics, and information operations in support of the Sahwa effort.[16] Essentially, by providing combat support and personal security, U.S. forces made the area safe, providing the shield which enabled the Sahwa to wield its sword against Al-Qaida at the level where it could make a unique contribution.

U.S. strategy took advantage of the Sahwa's strengths: their knowledge of the local physical and human terrain; their ability to identify and isolate suspected Al-Qaida members (whether outsiders or fellow-tribesmen); the presence of ready-made tribally-based cohesion; collective responsibility (despite rifts in ideological loyalties even within families); and the permanence which made possible continuous control of an area, taking away Al-Qaida's mobility and initiative, so that it became very difficult for the latter to operate without at least a tribe's indifference. Equally important was the Sahwa's ability to find Al-Qaida arms caches, the loss of which limited Al-Qaida's ability to move at an operational level.

Sahwa operations against Al-Qaida often took the form of struggles within individual tribes, pitting pro and anti-Al-Qaida tribesmen against each other, as Al-Qaida had also recruited from within the tribes. In fact, a local Sahwa commander noted that "most of those we arrest or kill are from our own tribe."[17] Pitched battles were rare, though there were some fierce armed engagements between Sahwa forces, often supported by U.S. combat forces, and Al-Qaida. More frequently, however, the dismantling of Al-Qaida's structure took the form of identifying and isolating operatives within a tribe — a task which only their tribe was capable of doing — and informing the authorities, turning them over, or eliminating them directly. As part of the anti-Al-Qaida fight, according to one shaykh, he had personally reported to the authorities 130 members of Al-Qaida from within his tribe, including an Al-Qaida deputy commander and a minister in Al-Qaida's ISI, which also suggests the depth to which Al-Qaida had penetrated into the tribal fabric.[18]

Sahwa casualties in the war against Al-Qaida were not negligible, with the Sahwa of Diyala province, for example, suffering over 1,000 casualties fighting against Al-Qaida.[19] Sahwa leaders also paid a price, as in the 2006-07 period alone, 28 prominent tribal figures were killed.[20]

The Sahwa Experiment – A Resounding Success.

Using any measure of success, the results of the Sahwa operations, in cooperation with Coalition forces, were impressive. In Al-Anbar, as General David H. Petraeus, Commander, Multi-National Force-Iraq, noted, "A year ago the province was assessed as 'lost' politically. Today, it is a model of what happens when local leaders and citizens decide to oppose Al Qaeda."[21] Monthly attack levels in Al-Anbar had declined from some 1,350 in October 2006 to a bit over 200 in August 2007 and, during the same period, 4,400 arms caches had been discovered, some 1,700 more than had been discovered in all of the preceding year.[22] By the summer of 2007, Al-Anbar had been largely secured, and Shaykh Ahmad Abu Risha estimated that there were only 200-300 Al-Qaida operatives left in the province by November of that year.[23] By early-2008, in Al-Anbar, the Coalition was able to begin transitioning control to Iraqi forces.

Al-Qaida itself acknowledged not only that it had suffered a bruising defeat, but also assessed that the Sahwa had become its biggest threat. It even claimed that the creation of the Sahwa had saved U.S. forces from "a disaster."[24] As an adaptive organization, Al-Qaida Central sought to analyze what had gone wrong in Iraq, producing a comprehensive policy review in late-2009/early-2010.[25] So impressed was Al-Qaida with the Sahwa that the document proposed to its affiliate in Iraq a counter-Sahwa, however unrealistically, urging: *"We call on the Islamic State of Iraq to establish jihadi Sahwa Councils."*[26] (emphasis in the original). Rather than railing against tribal loyalties as had earlier been the case, Al-Qaida now saw local tribal forces who were protecting their homes and their folk — but not necessarily commited to Al-Qaida's beliefs — as their best hope for control of an area. They saw that "these tribal units draw their power from their local environment, since they represent everyone in the area which they are defending and protecting."[27] Although modeled on the Sahwa, in Al-Qaida's case, these units were to have a jihadist orientation.

Al-Qaida's intelligence chief, likewise, drafted a paper in April 2012 dealing specifically with the Sahwa. He acknowledged that the Sahwa in Iraq "clearly had an impact on the jihadist movement" and that the Sahwa in general "is a new phenomenon for the followers of the jihadist movement, one with which they had not been accustomed to dealing."[28] Both analyses contained doctrinal guidelines for the future focused largely on dealing with the population with a greater degree of flexibility and realism in order not to alienate potential tribal supporters into being receptive to a Sahwa in any theater.

The Case of Iraq: Phase II.

Barring a foreign patron's unlikely intent to remain on the ground indefinitely or the eradication of Al-Qaida, inherent in a Model 1 tribal militia, is an inevitable Model 2, in which the local government now plays the role of patron, as was the case with the Sahwa in Iraq. As part of the phased handover of responsibility for the Sahwa from U.S. forces over the December 2008-April 2009 period, the identity of the governing authority changed for the Sahwa from the United States to that of a local player—the Iraqi government, with significant implications for the Sahwa's role and for the security situation in the country.

The Sahwa and the Iraqi Government:
A Rocky Relationship Benefits Al-Qaida.

A Clash of Political Cultures: Centralization vs. Decentralization. The tribes' quest for power and autonomy, supported by their ready-made Sahwa armed muscle, was bound to make any partnership with the Iraqi state an uneasy one at best, and even more so because of sectarian friction between the tribes in the Sunni areas and the predominantly Shia-based central government and military. Realistically, given the country's political culture, any Iraqi state is predisposed to centralize power and would look at a phenomenon such as the Sahwa—or at the factor of assertive tribes which lay behind the Sahwa militia—with concern as an active or potential threat. This relationship would have been difficult even without the presence of Al-Qaida, and the result has been an operational environment that is more favorable for Al-Qaida by engendering potential critical vulnerabilities which the latter could exploit.

The Iraqi government was never comfortable with how the Sahwa had been established and how it functioned independently with the United States, thereby sowing the seeds of mistrust from the start. A Shia journalist, perhaps reflecting government views, expressed his misgivings about the Sahwa early. He drew attention to the fact that the Sahwa's creation had bypassed the nascent Iraqi government in an extralegal move and that arming Sunni tribes would weaken the government in the long run.[29] A press report, citing unnamed "sources close to the Iraqi government," had called President George Bush's visit to the Sahwa leader Shaykh Abd Al-Sattar Abu Risha in September 2007 "a not very friendly signal, which contradicted protocol and embarrassed the politicians who were brought in after midnight to meet with the U.S. President in the strongholds of the tribal militias."[30] The Iraqi government was reportedly angry that the U.S. Government had not even informed it when an invitation had been extended to the Anbar Sahwa leaders for a visit to the White House in 2007, as the Iraqi Prime Minister's adviser for tribal affairs, Karim Bakhati, noted in a thinly veiled rebuke that "one would have thought that [the invitation] would have been sent through the Iraqi government," and concluded that "sending invitations in this manner bypasses the authority of the central government."[31]

The Sahwa expected to be treated as an equal player, alongside the government and the U.S. forces for, as a leading shaykh in Al-Anbar stressed, "We are not government employees."[32] At times, Prime Minister Nuri Al-Maliki was interested in developing ties with the Sunni tribes, as was the case before the March 2010 elections. That proved difficult, however, as shaykhs in one meeting with his representative expressed skepticism about his intentions. The fact that the meeting was also attended by U.S. military officers ensured some civility, but the government representative's assertion that "The Sahwa was imposed on us because of the security situation" and his rhetorical question,

"Does the Sahwa have any legal standing?" high-lighted the lack of mutual trust.[33] Mistrust continued to set the tone for the government's handling of the Sahwa. When the author asked a senior Iraqi military officer in 2012 about the current state of the Sahwa, he replied "We didn't want them," and expressed resentment, saying that they were a drain on the Army's budget— "you force us to pay [them]"—and insisted that the Sahwa personnel could not be absorbed into the military.[34]

(Mis)Managing the Sahwa and the Sunni Tribes. To make matters worse, the Iraqi government mis-managed its dealings with the Sahwa and with the Sunni tribes in general after the U.S. handover. It tried to marginalize the Sahwa, thereby alienating many shaykhs and tribesmen and helping to create a more favorable operational environment for Al-Qaida. The result was a reduction of the Sahwa's force structure and a degradation of its capabilities.

Interruptions and irritations connected with pay (now handled by the Army) alienated fighters throughout the system and made them more receptive to blandishments by Al-Qaida. In some cases, as in Diyala, pay to 4,500 Sahwa fighters was interrupted for more than a year.[35] Some Sahwa fighters simply walked off the job to protest late pay, such as those who abandoned their checkpoints in Diyala.[36] Pay issues at times became so exasperating that Sahwa personnel in Baghdad threatened to rejoin Al-Qaida if the situation did not improve.[37] A former Sahwa commander from Ramadi complained that:

> What has been offered to the fighters in Al-Anbar up to the present has been paltry in comparison to the sacrifices they have made. Those who were wounded

or even permanently disabled fighting Al-Qaida do not have medical care.

He taxed government promises made in public as "electoral propaganda" and pointed to the "very low" pay of 120,000 dinars ($102) per month for Sahwa personnel, categorizing that as "sad."[38] Insufficient funding also affected operational readiness, as the commander of the Sahwa in Samarra complained in 2010 that "Ever since the transfer of responsibility to the Iraqi government, we have been suffering from a lack of support. . . . We are now obliged to buy our own weapons and ammunition."[39]

Allegations of government harassment, ranging from gratuitous harassment and humiliation on pay day to widespread arrests of prominent tribal shaykhs for crimes allegedly committed during the fighting against Al-Qaida, also generated anxiety and dissatisfaction among Sahwa personnel and within the Sunni tribes in general.[40] In Salah Al-Din province, Sahwa members accused the central security forces of stopping them routinely and accusing them of having belonged to Al-Qaida in the past.[41] Rumors of more forthcoming outstanding warrants for past activities — when many Sahwa personnel had been part of the insurgency — prompted hundreds of Sahwa fighters in Diyala province to abandon their posts, with one local Sahwa commander concluding that such unfounded arrests were just being used as "a weapon to eliminate the Sahwa."[42]

Another source of considerable resentment within the Sahwa and the Sunni tribes has been a perception that the government was not doing enough — or even cared — about the security of Sahwa personnel and their families. Al-Qaida, for its part, made the elimination of Sahwa commanders a priority. The government's decision to end the salaries of the Sahwa leaders' bodyguards in 2010 was a very risky move, as it increased the shaykhs' already high vulnerability to assassination attempts as the threats from Al-Qaida increased, thereby putting the entire Sahwa structure in jeopardy. The government relented only with reluctance, in an effort to retain the loyalty of tribal leaders, but agreed only to a palliative solution: they increased the shaykhs' salaries and paid for just three bodyguards for each Sahwa commander.[43]

Mishandling the Demobilization and Integration of the Sahwa. The government was especially wary that the Sahwa not become a parallel Sunni armed force, but the clumsy demobilization effort only further fueled discontent within the tribes. As part of the handover, Al-Maliki had expressed his concern at a press conference that the government needed to ensure it had a monopoly over armed force and announced it would limit Sahwa powers of arrest, while expressing the need "to close out the Sahwa file."[44] In contrast, Iraq's tribal leaders expected to continue playing a significant political role, believing they represent a dominant sector of society. The Sahwa's representative, Shaykh Thamir Al-Tamimi, posited that the Sahwa should be maintained as long as there was a security threat in the country, including from Shia and Kurdish militias—in effect, putting off the Sahwa's disbandment into the distant future.[45] The government's announced intention to disarm the Sahwa fighters and to limit gun permits was also unsettling, especially in light of the integral gun culture of tribal life. As one Sahwa leader, Shaykh Ali Hatim, noted defiantly:

We will not hand over our weapons . . . why should we hand them over? Is that not part of my worldview, just like I have my religion so also I have my weapons. That is, I believe that weapons are a part of who I am.[46]

Clearly, the Shia-based military and security forces did not favor absorbing Sunnis from the Sahwa. Soon disagreements surfaced as to what had been agreed, with the government spokesman reiterating that it had approved the integration of only 20 percent of the Sahwa fighters into the security services, while the Sahwa's advisor was adamant that the government had agreed to absorb all Sahwa fighters who met the requirements, while those who did not would be given government jobs elsewhere.[47] Government spokesmen, in veiled warnings, continued to emphasize that the Sahwa was set up without the government's approval and that it could, if it desired, "suppress the Sahwa account without fear," even if it had not done so up to now.[48]

Those Sahwa members who were integrated into the government sector were often dissatisfied with their experience. Members of the Sahwa preferred security jobs rather than those in the civil side of the government, which usually paid less.[49] As one former Sahwa fighter complained, despite having faced great dangers in the fight against Al-Qaida, "we are surprised by . . . the jobs [we received], which are not appropriate to our dignity and our capabilities . . . such as in the sanitation or agricultural components of the state sector."[50] Other jobs were also temporary at best and, reportedly, the civilian government sector even discharged many Sahwa fighters it had hired originally, citing their lack of qualifications.[51]

Sahwa forces became progressively depleted, not only by partial integration into the government sector but also by outright release and the voluntary departure of disillusioned fighters. From a peak of 118,000 Sahwa personnel in April 2009 (although there may also have been additional unofficial fighters), by October 2010 only some 52,000 fighters remained on the official rolls.[52] Eventually, the Sahwa was allowed to wither away in all but name due to government neglect, with a reported 30,000 members by early 2013, although the actual number of those present for duty — and demoralized and resentful fighters at that — was probably even considerably lower.[53]

Al-Qaida's Rebuilding Effort.

As noted earlier, Al-Qaida's reassessment in the wake of defeat led it to modify, at least in part, its policies to remove some of the irritants that had turned the Sunni tribes against it and had enabled the Sahwa. As part of a new carrot-and-stick policy, Al-Qaida continued to attack Sahwa commanders, while it reduced its direct economic competition with the tribal leaders. Al-Qaida shifted its revenue collection from trying to control convoys through tribal territory to collecting from urban end-point merchants. Al-Qaida also began accepting neutral tribes, reduced leadership roles for foreign jihadists, and placed less focus on enforcing strict Sharia. Finally they expressed an intent to avoid civilian casualties, and showed greater willingness to work within the tribal hierarchy instead of seeking to overturn it.

These efforts combined with the Iraqi government's hostility and neglect toward the tribes and the Sahwa gradually allowed Al-Qaida to regain its former influence in the tribal areas. In particular, Al-

Qaida had an opportunity to draw away disillusioned Sahwa fighters by offering material incentives, and one Sahwa commander in Bayji warned that "Al-Qaida is spending large sums of money in order to attract back Sahwa members."[54] In the northern part of the Baghdad region and in Diyala, some 15 percent of the Sahwa fighters were said to have reverted to ISI by late 2010.[55] One Sahwa commander urged the government to rehire the Sahwa veterans who had been dismissed, with the specific purpose of preventing ISI from recruiting them again.[56]

Thanks to the mounting hostility against the government, ISI penetrated some Sahwa units, especially as many former ISI members had joined the Sahwa as a refuge after the U.S. victories. In the Abu Ghraib area, so great was the official mistrust of the Sahwa that the security forces refused to share intelligence with the local Sahwa.[57] In Diyala, some fighters serving in the Sahwa simply stopped cooperating with the authorities; according to the province's security forces commander, "They are not telling us if Al Qaeda is in the area. They are not warning us . . . A lot of them are definitely helping the insurgents."[58] In at least some instances, even before the U.S. withdrawal, the local Sahwa might cooperate with U.S. forces during the daytime, but then there would still be gunfire and rockets directed at U.S. bases at night, indicating that the Sahwa at the very least was not always reacting forcefully to the ISI presence, if not actually cooperating with the latter, as a way of hedging its bets.[59] Over time, Al-Qaida was able to rebuild its presence in many Sunni areas, reestablishing camps, continuing its harassment attacks against recalcitrant Sahwa commanders and mounting small-scale operations—and the occasional spectacular one—against government targets.

Tribal Revolt, the ISIS Onslaught, and Rehabilitating the Sahwa.

By 2010, general dissatisfaction had mounted in the wake of the continuing deterioration of the economic situation and the growing resentment in the Sunni areas thanks to government neglect and political marginalization. Even an individual in Al-Ramadi who had suffered earlier at the hands of Al-Qaida now complained. His comments reflect a general disgruntlement with the status quo:

> Everything has turned sour for us now. There are no services; we don't have jobs; poverty is killing us. What are they waiting for? Do they want us to beg in the streets so that we can live? Is that what they're waiting for?

And, he warned, "By God, if there is no change blood will flow ankle-deep and violence and killing will return once again to this province."[60]

The excessive use of force in a government crackdown against protesters in Al-Anbar in December 2013 catalyzed an open rebellion by many of the Sunni tribes, whose fighters soon named themselves the "tribal insurgents." Although violence increased in most Sunni areas, the epicenter of the dissidence was in Al-Anbar province.

Sunni — often Bathist-based or nationalist-religious — insurgent groups reemerged. More importantly, the recently-proclaimed Islamic State in Iraq and Syria (ISIS), as the continuation of Al-Qaida in Iraq — but now, as noted earlier, a dissident offshoot from the traditional central Al-Qaida leadership — also exploited the situation to make a spectacular comeback. Although the Sahwa may have been willing to oppose ISIS—even if not out of love for the government—some tribes now saw also ISIS as a useful, if distasteful, ally against an even more distasteful central government, while still other tribes remained neutral.[61] The government even accused some in the Sahwa, such as in Babil, of being passive "spectators collecting salaries."[62] ISIS, for its part, tried to deter tribesmen from participating in the Sahwa by decapitating or hanging the Sahwa fighters it captured, They also took reprisals against the families of Sahwa commanders. Many Sunnis, in fact, have continued to see ISIS as a counterweight to a hostile government or to Shia militias (or even to Kurdish forces in certain areas), a factor that ISIS has stressed, thus making the Arab tribes more willing to cooperate with ISIS.[63] (See Figure 1.)

Benefiting from the combat experience and equipment acquired fighting against the Asad regime in neighboring Syria, ISIS (known in the local sources by its Arabic acronym DAISH) was able to transfer some forces from the latter and to take advantage of Sunni discontent with the central government and of the Iraqi Army's critical vulnerabilities. In the campaign that unfolded, ISIS was able rapidly to take many of the towns in Al-Anbar as well as in other provinces and, in the process, to cause significant casualties and embarrassing defeats to the country's security forces.

As the security situation worsened, a beleaguered government hurriedly tried to reconstitute the depleted Sahwa, relying on Al-Anbar's fragmented system of tribal rivalries to find support against ISIS even if only among part of the population. Baghdad quadrupled Sahwa salaries to $430 a month for fighters in May 2013 and, the following month, allocated $130 million to finance the Sahwa through the rest of the year.[64]

Note: Figure 1 denotes an ISIS cartoon reminding Iraqis they need it (ISIS) for protection against the government. Local resident earlier telling ISI fighter to leave, but later regretting that now the area was at the mercy of the Iraqi government. Frame 1: "All of you leave our hamlet. It's our hamlet and we will defend it." Frame 2: "Help! The mujahidin have left and are allowing the government to butcher us!"

Source: *Al-Minbar Al-Ilami Al-Jihadi* Al-Qaida website, January 2014.

Figure 1. ISIS Cartoon.

In a 2013 recruitment campaign 10,000 new personnel, eventually rising to 16,000, were added to the Sahwa rolls.[65] The government also began to provide help with organization, logistics, equipment, and arms.[66] Some tribes, however, continued to hedge their bets, with their fighters working in the Sahwa during the daytime and with the insurgents at night.[67]

However, no doubt concerned about creating a future threat, the government remained reluctant to establish Sahwa maneuver units, despite requests for that, preferring the Sahwa to continue operating as small groups.[68] In an effort to try to consolidate command and control, and playing on tribal and personal rivalries, the government engineered the replacement in February 2013 of long-time Sahwa commander Ahmad Abu Risha by Wisam Al-Hardan, a tribal shaykh with fewer connections in the Gulf, who was seen as more cooperative with the government. By early-2014, the security situation had deteriorated further, and the government felt it necessary to increase the inducements to the Sahwa, promising $1 billion for reconstruction in Al-Anbar (although some estimates placed the amount of damage in Al-Anbar at $20 billion by May 2014), the future absorption of 10,000 Sahwa personnel into the security forces, and increased operational support in the form of air power and artillery.[69]

However, in the new operational and political environment, the Sahwa's success is less likely than when the Americans had been in charge. Currently, the Sahwa is no match in the field for the reenergized Al-Qaida with its recently-developed combat capabilities.

Relying on advanced weaponry (seized from Syrian Army arsenals or funneled to the anti-Asad rebels by foreign countries) and combat experience gained in Syria, in both urban terrain and conventional operations, they have developed effective maneuver units that use both mobility and surprise. These units' operations are backed by solid intelligence, well-developed psychological operations skills, solid plans targeting the adversary's weak points, flexible logistics, and even combat engineers. Thanks to these strengths, ISIS forces have continually out maneuvered and out-fought the Iraqi Army.

The Iraqi Army—plagued by faulty planning, lackluster and corrupt leaders, inadequate training, poor intelligence, neglect of the troops' basic needs, and inexperience in urban combat—was hard-pressed survive, much less to cooperate effectively with the Sahwa in meeting the ISIS challenge. Often, the Army was unable to seize and hold terrain, and usually resorted to inaccurate shelling and airstrikes along with other heavy-handed behavior that caused civilian casualties and damage that served as a further cause for Sunni discontent.[70] Some critics contended that some Army commanders were still reluctant to operate with the Sahwa due to sectarian bias, while Baghdad's officials in Al-Anbar in late 2013 had actually opposed expanding the Sahwa.[71]

Army casualties mounted, which some unconfirmed Iraqi security reports placed at over 6,000 dead and wounded by May 2014, out of 28,000 engaged in combat.[72] By then, Sahwa commanders could only travel to Baghdad by air due to the insecure roads. Morale was becoming a significant problem, leading to desertions, with an Iraqi security source reporting a 30 percent failure to return to the front after home leave, requiring replacements to be deployed from other parts of the country.[73] By mid-June 2014, the

Army in many areas had literally disintegrated in the face of a far smaller enemy, abandoning its equipment and fleeing, even — as in the case of Mosul — before ISIS attacked. Over 500 senior Army officers were said to have fled to neighboring Kurdish territory dressed in civilian clothes.[74] Notwithstanding continuing rosy situation reports from the government as well as the Army calling the retreat from Al-Anbar only "a tactical withdrawal," it was hard to argue that a small ISIS contingent had routed a much larger Army force and that it had seized sizeable swathes of territory, including many cities. In their advance, ISIS also acquired additional weapons (including the arsenal of the disintegrated 3rd Division), money seized from banks, and freed detained jihadis. They also sought to establish control over dams and water supplies as well as oil facilities, in order to exercise greater power over the tribal areas in addition to an advantage on the battlefield.

Assessing Iraq's Phase II.

Iraq's Phase II, with the Baghdad government in control of the Sahwa, highlighted some enduring problems with the Sahwa model. Clearly, the handling of the Sahwa was far less effective that when the United States had been the Sahwa's patron. In general terms, Baghdad paid the price of neglecting the Sahwa against a background of alienating the parent tribes, something that could not be undone quickly or easily. On the one hand, the political interests — exacerbated by sectarian differences — of the Sahwa and of Baghdad, as the country's national government, were bound to clash in a way that was not the case with the United States, which operated on a short-term horizon and did not feel threatened by the autonomy and sectarianism of the Sahwa and its parent tribes.

In operational terms, the Sahwa was often misused. Lacking numbers (and no doubt reluctant to take heavy casualties), the Army at one point was considering sending in the Sahwa and police to retake Al-Falluja, although they were likely to be outmatched by a defending veteran Al-Qaida force.[75] Such militias cannot be considered a stand-alone maneuver element. Lacking as they do the necessary training and weaponry, they would likely be outgunned and outperformed by a proficient combat force such as Al-Qaida had become. The Sahwa is most effective in small-scale anti-guerrilla engagements and as a security force for consolidation operations. The Sahwa operates optimally with a regular force that can provide it with effective support in functions such as fires, logistics, command and control, and mobility, support which the Iraqi Army only slowly acknowledged as desirable but became unable to provide.

Nevertheless, even as late as mid-2014, the conditions that had provided the favorable background for the United States to develop the Sahwa were still in evidence. In its rapid advance with relatively small forces, ISIS had not consolidated its control over territory, often bypassing areas of secondary importance or those where tribes put up a stiff resistance. Also, as earlier, ISIS has been in an uneasy coalition with Bathist ex-officers, tribal insurgents, national-religious and moderate jihadists—allies who had joined recently as ISIS's success became apparent and, as before, friction soon arose among these disparate groups. Moreover, ISIS was still bent on imposing strict religious law (including banning soccer, burning down beauty salons, and enforcing modest clothing), as well as demolishing saints' shrines, pressuring local women into marriage, and executing perceived opponents.[76] As late as June 2014, prominent Sunni tribal shaykhs and mainstream clerics expressed a willingness to work with the government against ISIS provided Prime Minister Nuri Al-Maliki stepped down.[77] Resistance to ISIS by tribal forces, often raised on local initiative, continued in cooperation with the remnants of security forces in the field in mid-2014.[78] ISIS itself continues to view the Sahwa as a threat and has created special anti-Sahwa units, the "Sahwa Hunters." (See Figure 2.)

Source: An ISIS anti-Sahwa unit in Iraq's Kirkuk province, May 2014, available from *Al-Minbar Al-Ilami Al-Jihadi*, an Al-Qaida website.

Figure 2. "The Sahwa Hunters."

Although the possibility of mobilizing tribal militias continued to exist, the government appeared unwilling to adopt that option. Sunni tribal militias persisted in requesting arms, financial, logistic, and operational support from the government, into mid-2014, but little was forthcoming.[79] Tribal militiamen in Al-Anbar, for example, complained in late June-2014 that they received no guidance or weapons or other support from the Army, which they accused of withdrawing and abandoning them to face ISIS alone.[80]

When the government did encourage new tribal militias, as the ISIS threat approached the Shia heartland, the focus was mainly among the Shia tribes in central and southern Iraq, with a smattering of Sunni tribes in mixed areas. While some Shia militias continued to be organized within party and religious brotherhood structures, the Shia response was now along tribal lines. It is claimed that 250,000 have volunteered for service, especially after the senior Shia cleric, Grand Ayatollah Ali Al-Sistani, issued a fatwa in June 2014 designating such service as a religious duty.[81] Each tribe established a volunteer recruitment center, while in Baghdad, tribal meeting houses served as mustering centers for the new militiamen coming from outside the capital.[82] The outpouring of Shia support, and the Shia Sahwa's promises that it would operate in and retake largely-Sunni areas such as Mosul and Salah Al-Din province, along with Prime Minister Al-Maliki's declarations that he would liberate Al-Anbar, no doubt only alienated many Sunnis further.

Conversely, with increased government dependence on tribal fighters in the Shia community, demands for enhanced political power quickly also emerged among the newly-established Shia Sahwa. In turn, the tribal Sahwa in the Basra area demanded the creation of a stand-alone ministry for a "National Guard," which may make Prime Minister Al-Maliki uncomfortable.[83] Moreover, government talk of incorporating the new volunteers into the Army — albeit as distinct units — was met within the Army with little enthusiasm, as it assessed the often over-age, out-of-shape, and untrained manpower pool as unsuitable for conventional military operations.[84]

As of mid-2014, although the situation remained fluid, Baghdad indicated that the government would no longer prioritize building a more effective relationship with the Sunni community or the Sunni Sahwa. They believed these efforts would entail a significant restructuring of the current Iraqi political system and a devolution of some powers from the center to the parent Sunni tribal areas. While Prime Minister Al-Maliki could try to reverse the major defeats suffered on the ground with a renewed military effort buttressed by the help of foreign advice and support, it is more likely that he may decide to focus instead on the Shia core areas, which contain both the bulk of Iraq's oil reserves and the only outlet to the sea, and which would enable him to consolidate his own power, rather than working to secure all or parts of majority-Sunni areas to the north of Baghdad for strategic reasons.[85] Even in case of the country's *de facto* partition, significant instability and conflict are likely to persist for years, especially with no clearly defined borders and many mixed and disputed areas. This is even more likely because ISIS has become overconfident, imbued with "victory fever" pursuing maximalist goals. However, even if, as seems likely, the Baghdad government has squandered its opportunity to work with a Sunni tribal militia movement to counter the ISIS, that failure does not invalidate the potential utility and even necessity of developing and using such a capability in dealing with Al-Qaida and its offshoots.

MODEL 2

The Case of Yemen.

Al-Qaida and the Arab Spring in Yemen.

The tribal militias that emerged in Yemen in the wake of the Arab Spring represent a Model 2 situation. That is, these militias have been the product of local initiative from the very first, with the Yemeni government acting as the managing patron of the militias established to fight Al-Qaida. These militias have been *de facto* tribally-based militias, recruited and deployed as tribal units, and used most often (although not exclusively) on their own tribal territory.

The Arab Spring in Yemen, more so than in other countries, was not so much a protest movement in favor of reform but, more a struggle for power between the ruling regime and competing forces that were often similar in outlook but differed in their tribal, regional, or religious affiliation, and were buttressed by personal ambitions. In relation to Al-Qaida, the Arab Spring set in motion events that eventually led to the downfall of the country's long-standing ruler, President Ali Abd Allah Salih. This was accompanied by the disruption of the established — if rickety — domestic balance of forces.

In Yemen, up to the beginning of the Arab Spring, Al-Qaida had engaged mostly in a low-level guerilla war using the typical insurgent tactic of hit-and-run attacks. By late-spring 2011, the advent of the Arab Spring, along with a concurrent challenge from the Shia Houthi rebel movement in the north, had a paralyzing effect on Yemen's government and military.

These circumstances apparently induced Al-Qaida to calculate that the time had come to escalate its operational goals and change its objective to one of setting up a state. As even a low-level Al-Qaida operative saw it, "We benefited from these revolutions. They gave us maneuver space. We were able to come out. . . . We were able to tell people about our mission."[86]

Al-Qaida now escalated its activities and began to carry out increasingly large-scale operations, leading at times to engagements involving large units, and often embarrassing the Yemeni Army and inflicting heavy casualties. In particular, Al-Qaida decided to concentrate its effort on where it could bring its greatest power to bear, namely in the Sunni tribal areas of the southern part of the country, where it had already been operating with mixed results and where there was an inherent mistrust of and sense of neglect at the hands of the government. For example, in Abyan province, the focus of its expanded activity, Al-Qaida reportedly was able to mass some 2,000 fighters by June 2011.[87]

In fact, boasting of having captured artillery, air defense guns, and tanks from the Army, Al-Qaida in September 2011 proclaimed in its official bulletin "the completion of the attrition phase against the Army." They meant that the first phase of the three-phase Maoist-based insurgency program which Al-Qaida had long internalized had been concluded, and that it was now appropriate to move up to the second, more advanced, phase of insurgency.[88] Al-Qaida also decided to expand its activity on the ground by seizing and holding terrain. True, Al-Qaida ran into tribal resistance in Dali province, an area that had long been a stronghold of leftist sentiment.[89] However, elsewhere, thanks to the weakened government and a reduced security presence, Al-Qaida was able to establish control in several towns during 2011, including Zunjubar, Jaar, Lawdar, and Shaqra in Abyan province, Rida in Al-Bayda' province, and Azzan in Shabwa Province. They even planned to advance on Aden itself, the largest city in the South.

Al-Qaida: Establishing a State and Creating Its Own Critical Vulnerabilities.

Al-Qaida saw the opportunity to establish quickly the nucleus of an Islamic state in Yemen. In fact, buoyed by its initial success, Al-Qaida now boldly and repeatedly proclaimed in its official bulletin that in the territories it controlled in the South, "we have laid down the first foundation on which to build the Caliphate."[90]

Al-Qaida's hasty expansion, however, may have been responsible for the rapid growth of the tribal committees that was to follow, as Al-Qaida's new prominence and the exercise of power in the towns it controlled generated tension with the tribal leadership.[91] In part, many tribes feared retaliation by the Yemeni military and by U.S. airstrikes for any Al-Qaida presence in their areas, a factor of which Al-Qaida was acutely sensitive. As its legal representative acknowledged, one reason Al-Qaida felt it was unable to spread further in Yemen was because the local population was afraid that it would attract air strikes.[92]

Despite the popularity of the social services and security that Al-Qaida introduced, the cost was clearly high. This was especially true in terms of Al-Qaida's enforcement of its vision of an Islamic society, which often led it to come into conflict with the local population. As long as it had military superiority in an area, Al-Qaida was able to impose its harsh model of society. Special attention was devoted to "Islamizing" the educational system, and the sexes were now strictly separated in schools. In the town of Azzan, music was forbidden in public areas, shop owners were told to grow beards, women were not permitted to work outside the home, and television and magazines were banned.[93] In one town, Al-Qaida attacked a wedding party and smashed the musical instruments being used in the festivities.[94] Al-Qaida also cracked down on alcohol and drugs, imposing harsh Islamic penalties, as was the case of a hashish user who was flogged.[95]

Al-Qaida, also sought to stamp out what it calls "sorcery" and "deviance," catch-all terms for what are in reality deeply-entrenched features of traditional folk religion. In Yemen's case, such practices as the veneration of saints and their tombs and of living holy men as the medium of intercession, mystical sufi brotherhoods, talismans, curses, incantations, and fortune tellers are widespread. In fact, Al-Qaida, while in power, was proud to announce initiatives such as their arrest of a "sorcerer" in one town, and it resumed the campaign with the August 2013 declaration of war against sorcerers and their pursuit, especially in Hadramawt province.[96] However, at times, Al-Qaida met with spontaneous resistance, as in the case of the attempt to suppress one "sorcerer" in Rida, which led to a lethal shootout between the latter's followers and Al-Qaida personnel.[97]

More generally, the rapid imposition of the Sharia to replace the more flexible and familiar traditional tribal law also created more than its share of friction with the tribesmen subjected to it.[98] No doubt tribal leaders often saw Al-Qaida's presence as a direct challenge to own their authority within their tribe, not least with the replacement of tribal law (in which the tribal shaykh and notables would have considerable influence and which would be a source of power and material gain for the tribal notables) by the Sharia. As Al-Qaida's Amir, or leader, in Abyan province, Jalal Al-Marqashi, acknowledged, his organization had tried to negotiate an agreement in one town with the local Popular Committees, but the stumbling block was Al-Qaida's insistence on the implementation of the Sharia, which the Popular Committees had rejected categorically, asserting "We cannot apply the Sharia in the town!!"[99] Local people reportedly also grumbled that punishments were handed out arbitrarily, without adequate investigations.[100] Even some of their initial supporters were said to have become disillusioned by the harshness of Al-Qaida's rule.[101]

Establishing the Popular Committees.

The Yemeni Army had already experimented with tribal militias in the South even before the country's new government came to power. The concept that had been pioneered by the Egyptian Army to fight against the ousted Yemeni royalists after the 1962 Revolution was revived more recently in the government's fight against the Shia Houthi movement in northern Yemen. It was a military factional leader, Staff Major General Ali Muhsin Al-Ahmar, then commander of the now-dissolved 1st Armored Division, who deployed Army units under his command into Abyan province and organized the official Popular Committees there in June 2011, although the committees he supported haphazardly were unsuccessful in the fight against Al-Qaida.[102]

To fill the vacuum resulting from the paralysis of the government as protests mounted in the capital against President Salih, some local leaders had also began to establish Committees in mid-2011, largely to regulate prices for staples or the distribution of essentials such as propane.[103] At first, such spontaneous Committees often cooperated with Al-Qaida, as when the latter took the city of Jaar from the Army in 2011, but soon disputes emerged.[104]

However, with encouragement and money from the new government, additional official Committees were now set up, often by government order, and many tribal leaders in Abyan and Shabwa provinces were quick to respond, with the specific intent of countering Al-Qaida. Tribes in Yemen are traditionally already well-armed, not only with personal weapons and rocket propelled grenades, but also with crew-served systems such as armor, artillery, multiple rocket launchers, mortars, and truck-mounted anti-aircraft guns used in a ground mode. However, in operational terms, the tribes on their own, isolated in their narrow arena, found it hard to compete militarily with Al-Qaida. The latter enjoyed the same advantages of familiarity with the local terrain, but also had the ability to move and mass over wider territories, thanks to a cohesive force structure. They even had gained artillery after their initial defeats of the Yemeni Army.

Perhaps the key inducement from the government side was the money that the latter provided to the Popular Committees. The shaykhs commanding the Committees became the conduit for the salaries and now, once again, it was the tribal shaykhs and notables who settled disputes among their fellow-tribesmen, rather than Al-Qaida's Sharia officials, thus restoring their usurped authority and providing them with additional political and financial resources.[105] For ordinary tribal fighters, the new salary—ranging from $60 to $150 a month, depending on the locality, plus food—is a princely sum in a country where that is equal to the average salary for a teacher and where over 54 percent of the population lives in poverty on less than $2 per day. In a country where unemployment is rampant, it is not surprising that most of the Committee fighters were drawn from the unemployed youth, often no more than boys.[106]

With the implicit delegation of control of an area to Committees and the absence of a government presence, the temptation also increased for the Committees to take advantage for their own benefit. There were complaints of arbitrary arrests, punishments, and executions, including the fatal flogging of one Army soldier they arrested for drinking.[107] According to one of the founders of the Committees in Abyan, the local population began to call Committee members "thieves and highway robbers" after the latter looted government property when Al-Qaida left in 2012. Committee members have often been accused of extorting money from truckers and merchants, which was made easier after they had expelled two battalions of national police from the province.[108] The lure of plunder may also be an inducement to recruitment, as illustrated by the dispute that arose between the local government in one district and the Committees over the division of vehicles and weapons captured from Al-Qaida, while in other instances the Army and the Committees exchange mutual recriminations over the looting of refugees' houses.[109]

Taking the Fight to Al-Qaida.

In many ways, the situation in a number of tribal areas was ripe for a confrontation with Al-Qaida, but it was only with the establishment of a modicum of political stability at the center after Salih had been replaced by his deputy, Abd Rabbuh Mansur Hadi, in February 2012, that the central government was finally able to redirect more of its military and security forces to the areas affected by Al-Qaida and to make it feasible for the tribes to challenge Al-Qaida.

The Yemeni Army clearly has had a need for the Committees, as it is as much a political as it is a military actor. Not only is the Army the regime's principal mainstay but also, at the same time, it is a potential threat. It is rife with factional fragmentation that reflect rivalries for power and funding, often pitting its commanders against each other and the President. This results in a diminution of the Army's fighting effectiveness as military commanders at all levels are often working at cross-purposes with their peers. What is more, the Yemeni military has long fielded fewer forces than it carries on paper. One source reported that instead of the claimed strength of 450,000 soldiers there were only 150,000 on active duty. A case in point is the 111th Brigade which had only 600 men present for duty instead of the authorized 3,000.[110] This chronic manpower shortage has made it difficult to deal decisively with Al-Qaida. Also, the Army has not always been able to consolidate its gains. Instead, it has to withdraw forces from one area in order to deal with challenges elsewhere. This means that to move against a dissident tribe or the Shia Houthis in the North, it must walk away from problems with pro-separatists in the South. For example, despite appeals from tribal leaders in late-2013 that the Army retain its presence in order to provide security in Al-Mahfad district in Abyan province, the units in question had to be withdrawn in order to reinforce the understrength 111th Brigade and the 2nd Brigade of the Republican Guard, leaving the original area more vulnerable to Al-Qaida.[111]

The 2012 "GOLDEN SWORDS" Campaign.

In Operation GOLDEN SWORDS, the campaign conducted during the spring and summer of 2012, the Yemeni military and security forces were able to deal Al-Qaida a serious defeat and to erase virtually all its recent gains.[112] U.S. support and, in particular, airpower, played a key role in some instances. For example, according to Yemeni sources, U.S. drones were instrumental in the retaking of the town of Jaar, where they were successful in targeting the armor that Al-Qaida had seized earlier from the Yemeni Army.[113]

The Popular Committees played a key role in the campaign and, in some areas, the Committee contribution to the fighting appears to have been decisive. For example, in the fighting for the town of Lawdar, local assessments claimed that the Yemeni Army had been on the brink of defeat when the Committees stepped in to defeat Al-Qaida.[114] By June 2012, after hard fighting, Al-Qaida was forced out of all its positions in Shabwa, Al-Bayda', and Abyanprovinces. Sometimes this was accomplished by means of combat or, in some cases, such as in the town of Azzan, by agreement. In Azzan, Al-Qaida reportedly negotiated directly with the Popular Committees to arrange for a peaceful departure by its members before government forces could strike. It also preemptively evacuated all the other towns in the area that it had seized earlier.[115] To be sure, Al-Qaida's defeat came at a high human price for all players. For example, there were hundreds of dead locals in the Lawdar district, where the fighting extended over a 5-week period.[116] Likewise, to retake the city of Zunjubar in Abyan province, official sources placed Army and Committee fighter losses at 280, although that number may well have been considerably higher.[117]

Given the Army's shortcomings, the Popular Committees have proved to be a crucial asset in the fight against Al-Qaida especially since, according to a senior Yemeni security official, the Army is not welcome in the southern and eastern parts of the country, given the overrepresentation of Northerners in its command structure.[118] Moreover, the involvement of such local forces helps mitigate the image of the Yemeni government's dependence on the United States for support, which can compromise its legitimacy.

The Committees' Security Role.

Apart from contributing additional fighters in the field, what the Committees made available to the Yemeni military that the latter lacked was access to intelligence and familiarity with the local terrain. In addition, Popular Committees provide an irreplaceable capability of identifying and controlling individuals from their own tribe who would or have joined Al-Qaida. They can even deal with symbolic details such as banning Al-Qaida slogans on motorcycles.[119] Of perhaps even greater importance, the Popular Committees' permanent presence has been instrumental in hindering Al-Qaida's mobility and initiative, thanks to a well-developed sense of territorial possession and the checkpoints that the Popular Committees set up on their own lands, thus making a major contribution to local security. As one Yemeni assessment saw it, a key reason for the Committees' continuing effectiveness was that "each area is defended by its own sons, as each Committee exercises its control within its own geographic space . . . each on its own territory."[120] In fact, press reports claimed that once the tribes took over the checkpoints in Hadramawt province in December 2013, they proved more effective against Al-Qaida than the Army had been.[121]

Moreover, given the absence of a strong Yemeni police presence in many areas, the Committees have provided law and order, as well as anti-terrorism service, freeing additional government forces for the anti-terrorist fight. The Committees have often been responsible for identifying and detaining Al-Qaida personnel and thus preventing potentially-significant security incidents. There is also a record of thwarting many small-scale attacks, such as the case of the arrest of an Al-Qaida operative at a wedding ceremony in Abyan province found to be wearing an explosive vest.[122]

Al-Qaida's Resurgence and the 2014 "ARMED DETERRENCE" Campaign.

Despite the government's operational successes in 2012, the basic political environment in the country did not change in many ways. There was persistent in-fighting in the government and military, as well as multiple threats to the government, including the Shia Houthi movement in the North and the pro-separatist movements in the South, tribal dissidence, and a continuing neglect of many tribal areas in terms of services and political participation. This instability continued to provide fertile ground for Al-Qaida, which was soon able to rally and reestablish many of its lost positions, mounting embarrassing attacks on the government and security forces. Initially, Al-Qaida was forced to revert to a focus on clandestine activity and guerrilla operations characterized by low-level actions such as assassinations, kidnappings, small-scale ambushes, and car bombs, punctuated only infrequently by bigger attacks against government targets. By mid-2013, however, there was a return of a significant Al-Qaida military presence along with a sharp rise in the size and lethality of its armed attacks. This resurgence included strikes in the capital and against Brigade-sized bases that caused significant casualties and embarrassed the government.

Stung by the regeneration of the Al-Qaida threat, the Yemeni government decided on a large-scale campaign in the spring of 2014. They targeted two southern provinces — Shabwa and Abyan — where Al-Qaida had made the greatest inroads. Although the official Yemeni news releases were not always reliable, the government forces, which included both the Army and police, appeared to have made significant progress. This resulted in extensive Al-Qaida casualties and, progressively, the latter's loss of virtually all the territory it had controlled in those two provinces.

The Committees were an integral part of the 2014 campaign, featuring prominently in local news reporting. Abandoning the policy of neglect that had allowed the Committees to atrophy in many areas after the campaign of 2012, the government, according to one Yemeni source, now recruited 15,000 new Committee fighters. That caused a significant expansion of personnel—in reality and on paper—by the end of 2013.[123] At least one tribe provided a Committee force that was 600-strong for the 2014 campaign.[124] Units of over a hundred Committee fighters operating alongside the Army were not uncommon.[125]

Committee fighters were reported to have been instrumental in locating both Al-Qaida strongholds and refuges for the Army.[126] As press photos from the field show the Committees fought side-by-side with the country's Army and police—often out of their home areas—as light infantry in conventional operations, although the Committees had previously had no equipment or training for that role, apart from their assumed ability to shoot and endure harsh conditions. However, the fighters apparently were allowed to deploy only with their personal weapons. On at least one occasion, the poorly-armed Committee fighters complained about being thrown into an engagement after Al-Qaida had ambushed an Army unit.[127]

In addition, the Committees were used in clearing operations in urban areas and villages, and were particularly effective in house-to-house searches.[128] In 2014 as in the earlier campaign, the Committees sustained significant casualties. The battle for the town of Lawdar in Abyan province alone reportedly resulted in more than 120 dead and 300 wounded in the Committee ranks.[129]

Al-Qaida has continued to view the Popular Committees as particularly troublesome, given their competition with Al-Qaida for control of the same tribal population and has sought to delegitimize the Committees by labeling them "criminal gangs, highway robbers, and moral deviates" who serve foreign interests.[130] (See Figure 3.)

Note: Al-Qaida anti-Popular Committee poster in Yemen: "Traitors: America's Popular Committees in Lawdar," available from Al-Qaida websites, 2012.

Figure 3. Al-Qaida Anti-Popular Committee Poster in Yemen.

Al-Qaida has also focused its attacks on the Popular Committee leadership as a way to undermine their organizational effectiveness. This has resulted in the death of a number of prominent tribal notables, with one tribal shaykh commanding a Committee who has survived no less than seven attempts on his life. At the same time, Al-Qaida has appealed to the Committees' rank-and-file, as in an April 2014 communique, stressing the fact that Al-Qaida fighters came from the tribes too: "we are your brothers and sons, and the sons of the tribes." Al-Qaida argued that it was not in the tribesmen's interests to get involved in a protracted war and warned that it would fight against anyone who joined the Committees.[131]

Managing the Popular Committees.

Despite their valuable contribution to the fight against Al-Qaida, the Popular Committees in Yemen have proved to be both a blessing and a bane for the country's long-term stability and for the government.

Complicating Traditional Governing Challenges.

The government found managing the Committees a challenge. To be sure, dealing with the tribes had never been easy. However, the added presence of Al-Qaida as a rival and the Committees' new sense of entitlement for the sacrifices they were making in the fight against Al-Qaida made the situation even more complex. Moreover, the tribes' sense of empowerment was bolstered by the government's implicit admission of its weakness. By recruiting the Popular Committees it revealed its reliance on the tribes.

As events in Yemen repeatedly show, tribes are not inert actors. They have their own interests. A shaykh from a leading tribal confederation stated that, with regard to the war against Al-Qaida, "The tribes will do what they see as appropriate."[132] (See Figure 4.)

Note: Underlining the Yemeni tribes' control of territory, resentment at the Army's presence, and enduring friction with
the central government, a tribesman chewing the traditional mild *qat* narcotic, frisks a soldier at a tribal checkpoint: "Do
you have any weapons on you, soldier?" *Akhbar Al-Saa* (Sanaa),
December 24, 2013.

**Figure 4. Yemeni Poster Showing Soldier
at Tribal Checkpoint.**

The inherent tribal commitment to autonomy
meant sensitivity to being used as a tool by the government and there was an initial reluctance to come
into conflict with Al-Qaida. As the head of the co-
ordinating council of the Bakil, one of the country's
two main tribal confederations, stressed, "We are not
government employees who have to pursue Al-Qaida
suspects."[133] Moreover, support for separatism in the
South reinforced the government's ambivalence re-
garding the Popular Committees, which some in the

50

South indeed saw as the nucleus of a future southern army.[134] The tribes' general mistrust of the central government was reflected in the fact that, after the 2012 defeat of Al-Qaida, many of the tribes also wanted the Army to leave their lands.

Accounting for Overlapping Tribal Loyalties.

Competing loyalties within the tribes has presented a recurring challenge to the Yemeni government in dealing with the Committees. Although the government has promoted the idea that 70 percent of Al-Qaida in Yemen is composed of foreigners, such claims are highly dubious. By far, most members are of local origin, and it is not surprising that in some cases tribes may remain sympathetic to their fellow-tribesmen even if they belong to a jihadist organization.[135] Despite the conflict that has often arisen between Al-Qaida and tribal societies, traditional tribal loyalties at times have trumped political allegiances or ideological differences. Under the circumstances, it was not surprising that after Al-Qaida's defeat in Abyan and Shabwa in 2012 some of its personnel reportedly were able to simply melt back into their own tribes or even to join their tribe's Popular Committee for protection.[136]

The factor of tribal solidarity can complicate the situation on the ground. In a typical attack in Abyan province in September 2013, an Al-Qaida raiding party surprised an Army post being supported by local tribal Committee personnel and a 2-hour firefight ensued. According to press reports, Al-Qaida was able to withdraw without incurring any losses. Not only did the engagement underline the Army's poor intelligence about Al-Qaida, but also suggested the fact that locals very likely had helped the raiders to penetrate the area. As some tribes have remained sympathetic to Al-Qaida or at least neutral, following this raid the local tribal Committee felt it necessary to warn other tribes not to provide shelter to any of the withdrawing Al-Qaida personnel.[137]

Dealing with Tribal Expectations.

Tribal interests can translate quickly into grievances. In Yemen, they have often proved to be sources of friction, as dissatisfaction periodocally arose because of the government's treatment of the Committees in particular and the Committee's tribal communities in general.

Friction between the Committees and the government has surfaced repeatedly in relation to complaints about the continuing lack of government commitment, and may complicate the consolidation of the government's gains. The Popular Committees have often grumbled about insufficient support in terms of providing weapons. Some local observers suggest that the reason is that the government is wary of maintaining well-armed militias that could prove a threat to central authority.[138] Committee fighters have also complained that money from the government is funneled through their tribal shaykhs instead of directly to them. Apparently, thanks to this arrangement, tribal shaykhs have often resorted to creating "ghost fighters." This inflates the Committee rosters on paper for their own benefit and infuriates the fighters, who were said to have preferred that the money be used instead to add more of those who are unemployed—no doubt their kinsmen—to the rolls.[139] One Committee in Abyan province complained that the government had not provided support for the families of their comrades who had been killed or wounded as had been promised, and that the Committee had not received arms and vehicles, but had to make up losses from their own means. More broadly, the same Committee grumbled that the government only collected taxes but did not provide any services.[140]

The Yemeni press also released official documents that highlight the government's dysfunctional policy toward the Popular Committees, revealing that, at one point, the country's Ministry of Defense was receiving five million Riyals ($23,000) from Saudi Arabia to pay the Popular Committees every day, but that the actual disbursement to the tribes was only two million Riyals a day, with accusations that the rest was being diverted for personal use by government officials.[141] One can imagine that such reports helped fuel additional discontent against the government among Committee fighters.

Committee fighters unhappy about late or unpaid salaries have often blocked roads—one of the standard Yemeni protest methods—to highlight their discontent.[142] In one case, angry Committees in Shabwa province suspended their activity for a week in January 2014.[143] In February 2014, one Committee commander in Abyan province quit in protest to what he said was the government's lack of payment, a move which the other commanders in the province supported, threatening to do the same unless such problems were addressed.[144] Complaining that the government was ignoring its rights and not addressing its demands, at the height of the fighting, the Committee in Ataq, the capital of Shabwa province, called a 1-week strike in May 2014, suspending its field operations.[145]

Command and control issues for the Committees during the 2014 campaign proved challenging in the field for the Yemeni military. In at least one reported incident, the Committees in two districts of Abyan withdrew from an active front, complaining that they were not getting adequate food from the military and that the latter was controlling their movement.[146] According to other Yemeni press accounts, the military commander in this instance was glad to see the Committee return home, as he had narrowly escaped an assassination attempt by one of its members, and he feared that the force had been penetrated by Al-Qaida.[147] Other reports told of the Committees looting weapons and equipment from Army units reluctant to take the field.[148]

Moreover, the Committees believe the Yemeni government has assumed a responsibility to integrate their fighters into the security and government sectors. While the Yemeni authorities have indeed promised that these fighters eventually could be absorbed into the military, police, or civil service, it is difficult to find places for additional personnel either in the bloated government bureaucracy or the partisan and costly military and police. Some Committee personnel have protested the broken promises of government jobs by blocking roads.[149] Although the creation of the Popular Committees has helped absorb some of the unemployed youth in the tribes, this is only a temporary solution. It is also one that can generate a backlash if the cash-strapped government neglects or decides to discontinue financing the program, thereby providing Al-Qaida with a more benign operational environment, as occurred in Iraq under similar circumstances.

Some Southerners have also begun to resent what they feel is the Army's use of southern tribal personnel as cannon fodder in high-casualty out-of-area operations. They claim the government was willing to do so in order to spare northern lives and to weaken, if not eliminate, the Popular Committees. For example, as the 2014 campaign was unfolding, one editorial asked, "Why are the Popular Committees taking part in this campaign which is being described as a campaign against Al-Qaida in Abyan and Shabwa, since this is a job for the Army?"[150] The editorial further accused the government of hoping to see the Popular Committees' commanders perish in the fighting.

Significantly, the Committees are a newly-legitimized armed actor that enables tribes to more easily reject central government authority and, at the same time, undercut national unity. From the beginning of their existence, a number of clashes have occurred between the Army and the Committees, such as when the latter refused to hand over to the Army government buildings that Committee members had seized from Al-Qaida in Azzan in July 2012.[151] There, and elsewhere, security matters have often since been performed independently by both the Committees and the Army, including duplicate security checkpoints on the roads.[152] Confrontations over the authority to set up checkpoints have continued to occur and have sometimes led to armed clashes between the Committees and the Army, as was the case in Hadramawt province in January 2014.[153]

As part of the 2014 campaign, the Yemeni government also promised the tribes that it would provide more public services. For example, after the retaking of the town of Al-Mahfad, the visiting newly-appointed provincial governor announced "a new page," and promised that the government would restore communications, and bring electric power, water, and health services to the local population.[154] However, whether the Yemeni government, perennially short of cash and of experts, can meet such promises in a timely manner, or whether it wants to strengthen the hand of the tribes, remains in doubt. In fact, by June 2014, the local Committees and tribesmen in Abyan were already protesting against the government. They were angry that no compensation had been paid for the damage they incurred as a result of recent government operations against Al-Qaida, as well as the lack of improvement in the provision of public services.[155] Elsewhere, as in Radfan in Lahij province, the Committees closed roads in June 2014 as they demanded back pay, which had been interrupted for 3 months.[156]

Clearly, in 2014 Al-Qaida lost the towns it had controlled and was pushed out of the two affected provinces, suffering extensive casualties and equipment losses in the process. Yemen Minister of Defense Major General Muhammad Nasr declared by early-May 2014 that government forces had "broken the back of Al-Qaida" and would not stop until Al-Qaida had been eliminated entirely.[157] The operational success of the 2014 campaign notwithstanding, it may still be too early to judge whether the setback will translate into Al-Qaida's demise or simply become part of a sine-wave pattern in Yemen of defeat and regeneration for the latter. In fact, there were indications that Al-Qaida may have been repeating its earlier strategy of withdrawing to preserve its force structure and awaiting more suitable operational conditions. The Yemeni Army itself spoke of Al-Qaida's "wholesale flight," and some Al-Qaida fighters simply melted back into their tribes, as they had done after the 2012 defeat. A case in point: as part of a deal the tribes in one area brokered between the Army and Al-Qaida during the 2014 campaign, only outsiders were required to leave, while local Al-Qaida members could return home.[158] The bulk of Al-Qaida fighters seem to have redeployed to other provinces, such as neighboring Hadramawt, where there were existing safe-houses and camps, but also further afield as in Lahij, Ma'rib, and Ibb provinces, suggesting this was not a decisive campaign, with some Yemenis intimating that deals were made to allow Al-Qaida to withdraw.[159] At the same time, Al-Qaida was still able to continue launching mostly small and mid-scale strikes, including in the capital.

CONCLUSION AND RECOMMENDATIONS FOR U.S. POLICY

Conclusion.

Present indications suggest that Al-Qaida and its affiliates — Al-Qaida for shorthand here — will continue to seek to operate in tribal societies, and that challenge will require an effective counter. Based on the cases of Iraq and Yemen, the preceding analysis suggests the positive results of using tribal militias in the fight against Al-Qaida may be significant. Within the context of fighting against Al-Qaida, encouraging and supporting any armed local constituency — such as Iraq's tribes — may be a reasonable or even an unavoidable option at a particular juncture either for an outside power or a local patron in dealing with that insurgency. The establishment of such militias may reduce or even obviate the need for a large U.S. Landpower footprint that could be costly both materially and in political terms. The creation of tribal militias by or with the consent of local governments is most conducive to success, and the ultimate impact of such militias will depend on the local government's treatment of the tribal sector. Nevertheless, as is often true in the real world, this is not a panacea, and, based on past experience, there are cautionary guidelines to be remembered for the creation and function of such tribal militias that could make the difference between success or ultimate failure.

Each of the two models studied has political and military advantages and disadvantages, but one may not have the luxury of which option to select in a specific situation. Comparing Model 1 and Model 2 suggests some general conclusions:

In **Model 1** (as in Iraq — Phase I), an outside patron in control, acting as the *de facto* governing authority, may be able to exercise better command and control, ensure more efficient use of money and other aid, and prevent or moderate the tribal militia's use for sectarian purposes than might a corrupt or ineffective national government. An outside patron may be more effective than a national government that may itself be a political player and potentially hostile to the tribal sector, which it might view as a rival. At the same time, a lack of permanence may make it difficult for an outside patron to ensure that the achievements of the militias it supported will be maintained once it leaves. In some instances, this model may be the only option available in the absence of an effective national government to act as patron, as was the case in many of the Sunni areas of Iraq in the years after Saddam Hussein's fall.

In **Model 2** (as in Iraq — Phase II and in Yemen), with a foreign patron in a support mode and a national government in charge, the latter may have the advantage of credibility in offering permanent support to the tribal militias and their parent tribes, which a foreign patron, with its short-term horizon, ordinarily will not. This model may also be less sensitive for an emerging local government's legitimacy than a foreign patron would be. In this model, there is an inherent tension and mistrust between any government in the Middle East, traditionally prone to centralize control, and any armed tribal force that may seek greater autonomy and establishes the capability to do so. This paradigm is only superseded temporarily by a dire need to confront Al-Qaida, as demonstrated when the Iraqi government revived the Sahwa in 2013, despite its manifest discomfort with the Sunni tribes, in order to deal with a deteriorating security situation. In some cases, this may also be the only option available, as the United States may not be on the ground and in control of a country.

Recommendations for U.S. Policy.

Whether the United States finds itself in the role of the director patron of a tribal militia as in Model 1 or as a supporter of a local patron as in Model 2, there are several recommendations that can help it be effective and avoid potential pitfalls in planning and executing policy. U.S. policymakers must assess each theater individually and tailor the general concept of tribal militias accordingly. There is no single template. Each country differs in its tribal structure, social norms, history of interaction with the central government, and the character of the local Al-Qaida movement. Nevertheless, there are some commonalities and general guidelines that can make U.S. policy more effective.

In Model 1, with the United States as the direct patron of militias, it should:

- Understand the strengths and limitations of tribal militias and shape the latter's roles and missions accordingly. Tribal militias are most effective operating on their own territory. In particular, tribal militias have a good knowledge of the human and physical terrain in their own tribal areas, built up over generations. Tribal members have the linguistic skills, familiarity with customs, and personal acquaintance with individuals that enables them to identify outsiders and suspicious locals. They can be used for sensitive tasks such as searching homes in their own tribal area. Coupled with their permanent presence on the terrain, they can provide stability once an area has been made secure by heavier forces. As such, even after the major fighting has ended, tribal militias, in conjunction with the police, can play a positive role in controlling an area, and maintaining the general security that contributes to preventing an environment in which Al-Qaida could regenerate. Conversely, although potentially proficient in small-scale engagements, tribal militias ordinarily lack the armaments, training, and command and control for larger-scale conventional operations against a skilled and well-armed opponent as Al-Qaida can be at times, such as in present-day Iraq. Out-of-area operations may be risky for tribal militias, as they may be at a disadvantage in terms of familiarity with the terrain and social milieu, while increasing the likelihood of their engaging in plunder and other misdeeds against the residents outside their tribe.

- Support a tribal militia adequately in material terms. In most areas where Al-Qaida is operating, either the population traditionally has suffered economic and social neglect or is hurting now because of the instability. While some individuals will be motivated for ideological reasons, many others will be influenced by material needs. Funding must be sufficient to pay salaries that will attract tribal fighters, as well as to provide goods such as food and fuel, and social services to the fighters' tribes. As in Iraq, salaries, job-creating projects, provision of materiel and social services, can be basic elements ensuring a committed Sahwa. Such civil projects and services can be tied directly to the tribal militias. The deterioration of such support by the follow-on patron had negative consequences that proved difficult to overcome. Providing the militias with the military means is also necessary, including supplying arms, munitions, and vehicles at the appropriate level. The militias must have effective operational support from their patron in the form of U.S. forces, focused on such complementary capabilities as fires (air and ground), logistics, intelligence, information operations, and help with mobility.
- Provide effective protection for key tribal militia leaders from inevitable Al-Qaida efforts to eliminate them, which could have serious consequences for the effectiveness of a militia. Every effort should be made to convince the follow-on government of the need for that protection to continue. Otherwise, the lack of effective provisions for post-handover security may

reduce the readiness of tribesmen to join a militia against Al-Qaida, fearful of their subsequent abandonment by their patron. Understandably, Sahwa leaders were concerned about their own safety before the U.S. withdrawal, and Al-Qaida has continued to target such leaders and their families.[160]

- In what is frequently a fragmented tribal political environment, discourage the use of tribal militias in inter-tribal feuds and avoid becoming involved in inter-tribal and intra-tribal rivalries unless this impedes the effectiveness of the tribal militia. Tribes may well be divided on whether or not to support a militia and/or the national government, and individual tribes may also be fractured internally on this issue, as has been the case in both Iraq and Yemen. For example, in Iraq during Phase I, as one shaykh in Diyala province concluded:

    > The tribes are split between supporters and opponents of cooperation with the American forces in the latter's fight against Al-Qaida. Some of these tribes face accusations of treason for standing with the Americans.

    Even some tribes who disliked Al-Qaida apparently had an equal distaste for the Americans and would have preferred to deal with Al-Qaida on their own.[161] To become a player in local politics can create enemies without creating friends.

- Ensure that the U.S. management and use of tribal militias do not undercut an existing or emerging government's legitimacy. Insofar as possible, the United States should involve an emerging local government in decisionmaking on the tribal militias and U.S. support (financing, arming, training, intelligence sharing) is best carried out through the local government if feasible.

Even if successful in terms of increasing security, fielding tribal forces may lay the groundwork for longer-term consequences with which a local government will have to deal eventually. In particular, the arming and encouraging of any tribal group may raise the latter's expectations and demands for autonomy. As a result, the tribes, with a legitimate military force, may be more likely to challenge the development of an emerging government's authority, heightening the likelihood of future violence and for Al-Qaida to take advantage. More generally, over the long term, supporting a tribal system can impede or derail the development of a more stable civil society. Both in Iraq and Yemen, certain urban circles have continued to exhibit considerable hostility to tribal values and influence, seeing in the latter a pre-modern mode of thinking and way of life, and urban intellectuals sometimes criticize tribalism openly.[162] At least while under its tutelage, the United States should seek to discourage tribal militias from acting as an armed political player.

- Craft a realistic and effective demobilization plan and ensure it is in place when and if the need for such forces ends — whether U.S. forces are still in charge or whether authority has been transferred to the local government — to ensure the success achieved is not undone. The United States must convince the follow-on government of the importance that any explicit or implicit commitments for material support continue after a handover, and the United States must be careful about the promises it makes. At times, the inability to fulfill promises, as perceived by the locals, generated disillusionment within the Sahwa about the Americans. As one Sahwa commander put it:

> The Americans are duplicitous and treacherous, and dispose of papers they are finished with by burning them . . . Unfortunately, earlier, we were obliged to work with them in order to secure our area, not to protect their soldiers who were being killed on a daily basis by Al-Qaida . . . I advise everyone not to cooperate with them in the future, since their fate will be the same as that of the tribal Sahwa in Iraq.[163]

Such negative impressions could create potential reservations among the tribal populations in other countries about committing themselves to similar militias. As one Yemeni analyst observed, suddenly demobilizing and not integrating this force into the security forces could make the fighters feel like "hired guns," and they could well turn against the government.[164] As demobilization may add to the local government's long-term burden, the United States should assist even after a handover in order to ensure a successful process. In most cases, demobilization is not a question of just disarming tribal militias in the immediate post-conflict period. Most tribal societies have always been or have become armed cultures, especially when the central government had collapsed or was weak. (See Figure 5.)

Note: Highlighting the deep-rooted attachment of Yemeni tribes to their weapons, a little boy says: "I wish I were an automatic rifle so that Daddy would love me more and would always take me with him." See Kamal Sharq, *Al-Jumhuriya* (Sanaa), June 10, 2014.

Figure 5. Yemeni Tribal Cartoon.

In light of the culture and the real possibility of a continuing need for self-protection, it would be unrealistic to demand a relinquishing of personal arms and would be likely to elicit resistance. Instead, the focus should be on persuading the follow-on local government patron to integrate former tribal fighters into the security, government, and civil sectors if and when the Al-Qaida threat has been eliminated for good. To prepare for demobilization, the United States should take advantage of the security and time gained by a tribal militia's success to build local government capacity. This will help to ensure the emergence of a stable and effective domestic authority able to assume control of the country and the militia, if the latter is still needed. Otherwise, a tribal militia left in control of an area and lacking government supervision could well lead to abuses against the civilian population.

- Conduct an effective information campaign directed toward the tribes. In particular, U.S. policy should focus on the enemy and be shaped to appeal to the tribes. This policy would take advantage of Al-Qaida's critical vulnerabilities in ideology and its relationship with a country's tribal base. Al-Qaida will seek to undermine the tribal militia's leadership and appeal to tribal fighters, promising money, playing on religious sentiments, kinship ties, shame about cooperating with an occupier and an "apostate" local government, It will also play upon fears that the foreign patron will abandon the militia and leave the fighters defenseless. (See Figure 6.)

Note: ISI poster against the Sahwa: "A Sahwa member will not get past the Islamic State of Iraq; there is no place among us for the Sahwa." Al-Qaida's Al-Luyuth forum, August 2011.

Figure 6. ISI Poster.

At a cruder level, Al-Qaida will intimidate tribal militias by threatening and carrying out assassinations, kidnapping, and attacks on family members. (see Figure 7.) Clearly, the United States needs to neutralize this strategy through both its own information effort and with tangible measures that invalidate such claims.

Note: ISI poster intended to intimidate the Sahwa and Iraq's other security forces: "This is the last thing a Sahwa member, a soldier, and an apostate policeman see in the Islamic State of Iraq," Al-Qaida websites, 2010.

Figure 7. ISI Poster.

Even in a **Model 2** situation, the United States can make essential contributions to the success of the tribal militias while avoiding direct involvement on the ground, and should:

- Provide funding, arms, selected operational support, intelligence, and advice — either in direct support of the local patron government operating jointly with the tribal militia or intended for the tribal militia but channeled through the patron local government. For example, in 2013, the United States supplied small arms to the Iraqi government and specifically urged the latter to transfer that equipment to the reconstituted Sahwa.[165] In the 2014 campaign in Yemen, U.S. support to the government forces came in the form of airstrikes, additional U.S. arms and equipment, and other U.S. direct operational support, including reportedly flying Yemeni commandos within the battle zone.[166] Although such support may not have been earmarked for the Popular Committees, it clearly also benefited the latter as they operated alongside the government forces. In another example of outside support, Saudi Arabia, as noted, has provided much of the funding for the Popular Committees in Yemen, funneling that through the latter country's Ministry of Defense. Riyadh has also provided medical evacuation for a key Committee commander in 2012.

- Advise the local government on how to best deal with the tribal militias. Recently, the U.S. administration conducted consultations with Iraqi leaders, suggesting strategy, urging outreach to the tribal leaders, and publicly praising Baghdad's decision to extend benefits to the tribal militias.[167] In 2014, the U.S. administration also publicly encouraged the integration of Sahwa fighters into Iraq's security forces.[168] In terms of supporting the Sahwa's patron in combat operations in 2013-14, the United States helped by having U.S. Special Forces train Iraqi Special Forces in Jordan and by providing advice, equipment, and intelligence, and reportedly launched drone strikes from Jordan against Al-Qaida targets.[169]

- Advise and support other countries that might act in the future as potential patrons of tribal militias' use a tool against Al-Qaida. Both Algeria and Mali, for example, have considered tribal militias, while France could become a sponsor in the Sahel.[170]
- Identify personnel from the U.S. Army and Marine Corps with operational experience working with tribal militias, and allow them to act as instructors for future U.S. operations and as advisers to allied efforts when they consider establishing such forces.

AN UPDATE

Since the time that this text was completed in the early summer of 2014, a new government, led by Haydar Al-Ibadi, replaced that of Prime Minister Al-Maliki in Iraq. A combination of a modified Army, Coalition airpower, and Kurdish and Shia militias has been successful in stemming the Islamic State's (ISIS) momentum but, although Prime Minister Al-Ibadi has a declared policy of accommodating the Sunni community, in many ways a hardening of sectarian positions has also occurred.

Significantly, as part of the fight against the ISIS, a U.S.-backed plan emerged for the establishment of a "National Guard" as a provincial force which will include current and former Sahwa fighters in trained maneuver units armed with heavier weaponry and meant to reassure Al-Anbar and other predominantly Sunni areas. Given the reality of the social structures of the intended areas, tribal loyalties and power relationships will still have to be considered. In effect, representatives from the United States and Iraq were said to be negotiating with Sunni tribal shaykhs on the parameters of this new National Guard, which is likely to resemble a "Sahwa-plus." At the same time, the retention of a more traditional Sahwa as a complementary local home guard with a permanent territorial security presence would also be useful.

In the meantime, a resolution of Sunni-Shia differences on the very need for a National Guard, as well as on its size, armament, mission, membership—including whether to also admit Shia militiamen—and its relationship to the Baghdad government and the national security forces is still pending. Ultimately, for the success of any Sunni-based force in the fight against ISIS, differences on such broader political issues as the role of the former Bath Party and officers from Saddam's army, the presence of resurgent Shia militias in Sunni areas, the appropriate use of government air power, the desirability of Coalition ground forces in Iraq, amnesty for tribal supporters of ISIS, and the reform of Army and police structures will still have to be settled. In whatever way the Sahwa concept evolves, the issues addressed above will likely still remain relevant for any tribally-based society and force.

ENDNOTES

1. The term "Syria" (hence ISIS)—really Greater Syria with still ambiguous borders—is preferable to that of "Levant" (or ISIL), a term historically not common in American English and equally ambiguous in its geographic extent.

2. For some studies of the tribal militias in Yemen and in Iraq, see Casey L. Coombs, "Yemen's Use of Militias to Maintain Stability in Abyan Province," West Point, NY: Combating Terrorism Center, February 20, 2013, available from *www.ctc.usma. edu*; "Tribal Militias in Yemen: Al Bayda and Shabwah," *Critical Threats*, February 7, 2013, available from *www.criticalthreats.org/ print/5153*; Michael Bush, "Militias, Sahwa and Shared Interests: Insights for Doctrine," *Small Wars Journal*, October 21, 2013, available from *smallwarsjournal.com/print/14769*; and Norman Cigar, *Al-Qaida, the Tribes, and the Government. Lessons and Prospects for Iraq's Unstable Triangle*, Quantico, VA, Marine Corps University Press, 2011, the main source on Iraq's experience.

3. "Asha'ir Al-Iraq tutalib bi-iqrar qanun khass biha" ("Iraq's Tribes Demand the Enactment of a Special Law for Them"), *Al-Sharq Al-Awsat* (London), October 14, 2012, available from *www. aawsat.com/print.asp?did=699701&issueno=12374*.

4. Shaykh Ali Hatim, Interview with Majid Hamid, Sinaat al-mawt (The Death Industry) program, "Ightiyal shuyukh al-asha'ir . . . al-fail wa-'l-asbab" ("Assassinations of the Tribal Shaykhs . . . the Perpetrator and the Causes"), Al-Arabiya TV (Abu Dhabi, UAE), February 1, 2007, transcript available from *www.alarabiya. net/save_print.php?print=1&cont_id=65493*.

5. Mushriq Abbas, "Tajadhubat asha'iriya wa-siyasiya rafaqat sirau ma al-qaida wa-'l-Maliki . . . Masira qasira wa-ghamida qadat Abu Risha ila jiwar Bush" ("Tribal and Political Mutual Attractions Accompanied His Struggle with Al-Qaida and Al-Maliki . . . A Murky and Short Journey Led Abu Risha to Bush's Side"), *Al-Hayat* (London), September 16, 2007, *international.daralhayat. com/print/155881/archive*.

6. Joe Klein, "Saddam's Revenge," *Time*, September 18, 2005, available from *content.time.com/time/magazine/article/0,9171, 1106307,00.html*.

7. Major Morgan Mann, USMCR, "The Power Equation: Using Tribal Politics in Counterinsurgency," *Military Review*, Vol. 87, No. 3, May-June 2007, p. 104.

8. See Anthony H. Cordesman, *Iraq's Insurgency and the Road to Civil Conflict*, Vol. 2, Westport, CT: Praeger Security International, 2008, pp. 474-480.

9. Shaykh Jasim Muhammad Salih Al-Suwadawi, Interview in Colonel Gary W. Montgomery and Chief Warrant Officer-4 Timothy S. McWilliams, eds., *Al-Anbar Awakening, Vol. 2, Iraqi Perspectives; From Insurgency to Counterinsurgency in Iraq, 2004-2009*, Quantico, VA: Marine Corps University Press, 2009, p. 70.

10. Shaykh Ali Hatim, Interview in *Ibid.*, p. 118. Actually, at $300 a month, the 54,000 Sahwa fighters in the Baghdad region would have cost about $16 million a month in salaries. According to General David Petraeus, the United States spent an estimated $35 million for all the Sahwa during 2007, *Iraqi Benchmarks; Hearings before the Committee on Armed Services, United States Senate, 110th Congress*, September 7 and 11, 2007, Washington, DC: U.S. Government Printing Office (GPO), 2008, p. 302.

11. Joshua Partlow and John Ward Anderson, "Tribal Coalition in Anbar Said to Be Crumbling," *Washington Post*, June 11, 2007, p. A11.

12. Major General John R. Allen, Interview in Chief Warrant Officer-4 Timothy S. McWilliams and Lieutenant Colonel Kurtis P. Wheeler, eds., *Al-Anbar Awakening, Vol. 1, American Perspectives; From Insurgency to Counterinsurgency in Iraq, 2004-2009*, Quantico, VA: Marine Corps University Press, 2009, p. 230.

13. According to James V. Soriano, Provincial Reconstruction Team Leader in Al-Anbar, *Ibid.*, p. 276.

14. Major General John R. Allen, *Ibid.*, p. 236.

15. Jim Michaels, "Behind Success in Ramadi an Army Colonel's Gamble," *USA Today*, May 1, 2007, available from *www.usatoday.com/cleanprint/?1291073743841*.

16. See, for example, Richard Schultz, *The Marines Take Anbar*, Annapolis, MD: U.S. Naval Institute Press, 2013; and Major Niel Smith and Colonel Sean MacFarland, *"Anbar Awakens: The Tipping Point,"* Military Review, Vol. 88, No. 2, March–April 2008, pp. 41-52.

17. "Al-Faqr wa-'l-jahl awamil ashamat fi tahwil qura min Diyala ila maladhdhat amina li-'l-Qaida" ("Poverty and Ignorance Are Contributing Factors in Transforming Villages in Diyala into Safe-Areas for Al-Qaida"), *Al-Sabah Al-Jadid* (Baghdad), May 27, 2009, available from *www.newsabah.com*.

18. Hadi Al-Anbaki, "Shaykh ashira fi Diyala yubligh an 130 irhabi min aqriba'ih baynhum qiyadat fi Al-Qaida" ("The Shaykh of a Tribe in Diyala Denounces 130 Terrorists from among His Relatives, Including Al-Qaida Leaders"), *Al-Sabah* (Baghdad), August 4, 2008, available from *www.alsabah.com/paper.php?source=akb ar&mlf=copy&sid=67273*.

19. "Khasa'ir sahwat Diyala fi harbiha ma al-tatarruf balaghat akthar min alf shahid wa-jarih" ("The Losses of the Diyala Sahwa in Its War against Extremism Has Reached More Than One Thousand Dead and Wounded"), Al-Sumarriya TV (Baghdad), September 30, 2010, transcript available from *www.alsumaria.tv./ ar/print-news-1-55169.html*.

20. "Al-Qaida tatawad bi-istihdaf shuyukh al-asha'ir wa-'l-mutarjimin wa-ula amaliyat al-tasfiya bada'at yawm ams al-awwal" ("Al-Qaida Threatens to Target Tribal Shaykhs and Interpreters and the First of the Liquidation Operations Began the Day before Yesterday"), *Al-Jiwar* (Baghdad), May 1, 2010, available from *www.aljewar.org/news-24059.aspx*.

21. General David H. Petraeus, *Report to Congress on the Situation in Iraq*, September 10-11, 2007, Washington, DC: GPO, 2008, p. 5, available from *www.defense.gov/pubs/pdfs/Petraeus-Testimony20070910.pdf*.

22. *Ibid.*, p. 4.

23. "Al-Shaykh Ahmad Abu Risha yakshif tafasil jadida an qatil al-shaykh al-shahid Abd Al-Sattar wa yanfa hurub qatilayhi min al-sijn" ("Al-Shaykh Ahmad Abu Risha Reveals New Details about the Martyr Shaykh Abd Al-Sattar's Killer and Denies That His Two Killers Have Escaped from Prison"), Wikalat Anba' Al-Buratha (Baghdad), November 20, 2007, available from *www.burathanews.com*.

24. Abu Ahmad Abd Al-Rahman Al-Masri, *Dawlat Al-Iraq al-islamiya haqiqa la awham, wa-waqi la ahlam* (*The Islamic State of Iraq Is a Fact, Not a Fantasy, and Reality, Not a Dream*), Sariyat Al-Sumud Al-Iilamiya, February 2009, pp. 136, 139.

25. *Khutta istiratijiya li-taziz al-mawqif al-siyasi li-Dawlat Al-Iraq Al-Islamiya* (*Strategic Plan Intended to Strengthen the Political Position of the Islamic State of Iraq*), Mufakkirat Al-Falluja, Muharram 1431, December 2009-January 2010.

26. *Ibid.*, p. 39.

27. *Ibid.*, p. 40.

28. Abu Ubayda Abd Allah Khalid Al-Adam (d. 2013), *Sahwat al-ridda wa'l-sabil li-maniha* (*The Apostate Sahwas and How to Prevent Them*), Markaz Al-Fajr li'l-Alam, April 8, 2012, p. 2.

29. Salah Bassis, "Taslih al-asha'ir" ("Arming the Tribes"), *Al-Sabah*, July 24, 2007, available from *www.alsabah.com/paper.php?source=akbar&mlf=copy&sid=46550*. To be sure, when the Sahwa was established later, also in Salah Al-Din province in 2007, this was done with greater coordination with the Iraqi government, which granted permission for the raising of such forces. Interview with Shaykh Ali Hatim by Muntaha Al-Ramhi, Panorama program, Al-Arabiya TV, September 16, 2007, transcript available from *www.alarabiya.net/programs/2007/09/1839267.html*.

30. Abbas.

31. *Ibid.*

74

32. Shaykh Ali Hatim , Interview with Ali Sulayman by Abd Al-Azhim Muhammad, "Al-Mashhad al-iraqi: Tajrubat taslih al-asha'ir fi al-Anbar" ("The Iraqi Scene: The Experiment of Arming the Tribes in Al-Anbar"), Al-Jazira TV (Doha, Qatar), July 29, 2007, transcript available from *www.aljazeera.net*.

33. "Shuyukh al-sahwa bayn mitraqat Al-Qaida wa-sindan al-hukuma" ("The Sahwa Shaykhs Are between the Hammer of Al-Qaida and the Anvil of the Government"), *Al-Sharq Al-Awsat*, January 25, 2009.

34. Discussion with the author, Washington, DC, March 7, 2012.

35. According to Ahmad Al-Mujammai, leader of the Sahwa in Diyala, "Ratib 4500 muqatil bi-Diyala tadur fi halqa mufragha wasat dawat li-tasrihhim" ("The Salary of 4500 Fighters in Diyala Is Caught in a Vicious Circle amid Calls for Their Disbandment"), *Aswat Al-Iraq*(Baghdad), August 21, 2010.

36. "Insihab majmua min muntasibi al-sahwat al-yawm al-arbia' min wajibhim fi mintaqat Baladruz ihtijajan," ("A Unit of Sahwa Personnel Pulls Back Today, Wednesday, from Their Duty Posts in the Baladruz Area in Protest"), *Wikalat Anba' Al-Mustaqbal* (Baghdad), February 9, 2011, available from *www.mustakbal. net/ArticlePrint.aspx?ID=1563*.

37. "Ahali Al-Azhamiya li'l-*Sharq Al-Awsat*: Al-Qaida tatarakkaz fi Shari' Al-Akhtal . . . wa tastaghill al-atilin" ("The Inhabitants of Al-Azamiya to *Al-Sharq Al-Awsat*: Al-Qaida Is Concentrated in Al-Akhtal Street . . . and Is Taking Advantage of the Unemployed"), *Al-Sharq Al-Awsat*, August 1, 2010, available from *www.aawsat.com/print.asp?did=580572&issueno=11569*.

38. "Qa'id sabiq li'l-sahwat yantaqid ihmal al-hukuma laha wa-mas'ul fi sahwat Al-Iraq yushir ila tahawwulha li-kiyan siyasi" ("A Former Commander of the Sahwa Criticizes the Government's Neglect of the Latter, While an Official of the Iraq Sahwa Indicates That It Has Been Transformed into a Political Body"), *Aswat Al-Iraq*, February 14, 2010, available from *ar.aswataliraq.info*.

39. "Al-Sahwa takhsha intiqam Al-Qaida bad insihab al-qu-wwat al-amirikiya" ("The Sahwa Fears Al-Qaida's Revenge after the American Forces Withdraw"), *Al-Hayat*, August 22, 2010, available from *international.daralhayat.com/print/174456*.

40. "Anasir al-sahwat yashkun qillat al-ihtimam al-hukumi bi-awdahim" ("Sahwa Personnel Complain of Government Lack of Interest about Their Conditions"), Qanat Al-Furat Al-Fada'iya TV (Baghdad), July 27, 2010, available from *alforattv.net/index.php?show=news&action=print&id=47072*.

41. Muhammad Abd Allah Muhammad, "Al-Sahwat wa'l-Qaida" ("The Sahwa and Al-Qaida"), *Al-Rafidayn* (Baghdad), November 4, 2010, available from *www.alrafidayn.com*.

42. "Sha'iat tanfiha al-sultat an mudhakkirat itiqal tu'addi ila ikhla' maqarr lil'l-sahwat fi Diyala" ("Rumors Which the Authorities Deny of Arrest Warrants Lead to the Abandonment of Posts by the Sahwa in Diyala"), *Al-Sabah Al-Jadid*, May 9, 2009, available from *www.newsabah.com*.

43. "Mustashar al-sahwat: hasalna ala muwafaqa ala ratib wa-himaya li-qadatna" ("Sahwa Adviser: We Reached an Agreement on Salaries and Protection for Our Commanders"), *Al-Sabah Al-Jadid*, May 5, 2010, available from *www.newsabah.com*.

44. "Al-Maliki yulin an ijra'at tamhidan li-ghalq milaff al-sahwat" ("Al-Maliki Announces Steps in Preparation for Closing Out the Sahwa File"), *Al-Sabah*, September 15, 2008, available from *www.alsabah.com/paper.php?source=akbar&mlf=copy&sid=69761*.

45. Thamir Al-Tamimi, interview in "Istihdaf al-sahwat" ("Targeting the Sahwa"), Baghdad Satellite TV (Baghdad), July 18, 2010, transcript available from *www.baghdadch.tv/news_special.php?id=1800&print=1*.

46. Shaykh Ali Hatim, Interview with Ili Nakuzi, "Ma Ali Al-Hatim al-qiyadi bi-sahwat Al-Anbar" ("With Ali Al-Hatim, the Anbar Sahwa Leader"), Al-Arabiya TV, February 3, 2008, transcript available from *www.alarabiya.net/save_print.php?print=1&cont_id=45115*.

47. Udayy Hatim, "Min haraka iraqiya musallaha ila tayyarat siyasiya" ("From an Iraqi Armed Movement to Political Factions"), *Al-Hayat*, November 16, 2008, available from *international. daralhayat.com/print/229160/archive.*

48. According to Muhammad Al-Askari, the Public Relations Adviser in the Iraqi Ministry of Defense, Layla Al-Shayib, "Ma wara' al-khabar: Sahb tarakhis al-silah al-tabi li-majalis al-sahwa" ("Behind the News: Withdrawing Gun Permits from the Sahwa Councils"), *Al-Jazira*, June 8, 2010, transcript available from *www. aljazeera.net.*

49. "Al-Sahwat yufaddilun al-amal al-amni" ("The Sahwa Prefers Security Work"), *Al-Sabah Al-Jadid*, April 14, 2009, available from *www.newsabah.com/tpl?IdLanguage=17&NrIssue=1401& NrSection=21&NrArticle=26363.*

50. "Anasir al-sahwat yashkun qillat al-ihtimam al-hukumi bi-awdahim" ("Sahwa Members Complain of Government Lack of Interest about Their Conditions"), Qanat Al-Furat Al-Fada'iya TV, July 27, 2010, available from *alforattv.net/index.php?show=news &action=print&id=47072.*

51. "Al-Musalaha al-wataniya tu'akkid hajat bad al-muha-fazhat ila khadamat Abna' Al-Iraq" ("The National Conciliation Committee Confirms That Some Provinces Need to Provide Services for the Sons of Iraq"), *Al-Wikala Al-Ikhbariya li'l-Anba'* (Baghdad), December 1, 2010, available from *www.ikhnews.com/popup. php?action=printnews&id=4992.*

52. "Sahwat muadiya." Other government sources placed the remaining number at 40,000. "Al-Musalaha Al-Wataniyya: Qariban ghalq malaff abna' Al-Iraq (al-sahwat)" ("The National Reconciliation Committee: Closing the Sons of Iraq [Sahwa] Account Soon"), *Al-Wikala Al-Ikhbariya Li'l-Anba',* October 7, 2010, available from *www.ikhnews.com/popup.php?action=printnews&id=2847.* (Hereafter "Al-Musalaha Al-Wataniyya.")

53. "Sa-nastain bihim li-himayat al-anabib al-naftiya" ("We Will Use Them to Guard the Oil Pipelines"), *Al-Mada* (Baghdad), May 4, 2013, available from *almadapress.com.*

54. "Al-Qaida tutliq hamla li-iqna rijal al-sahwa al-mutad-hammirin bi-'l-awda ilayha" ("Al-Qaida Launches a Campaign to Convince Disgruntled Members of the Sahwa to Rejoin It"), *Al-Sharq Al-Awsat*, August 7, 2010, available from *www.aawsat.com/print.asp?did=580572&issueno=11575*.

55. "Sahwat muadiya li-'l-Qaida taud ila al-tamarrud fi shimal Baghdad" ("Sahwa Hostile to Al-Qaida Returns to Dissidence in the North Baghdad Area"), *Al-Sabah Al-Jadid*, October 19, 2010, available from *www.newsabah.com*.

56. Hadi Al-Anbaki, "Tashkil khalaya istikhbariya fi Diyala li-ifshal khutat Al-Qaida bi-shira' al-dhimam" ("Creation of Intelligence Cells in Diyala to Abort Al-Qaida's Plans to Buy Protection"), *Al-Sabah*, August 7, 2010, available from *www.alsabah.com/paper.php?source=akbar&mlf=interpage&sid=106797*.

57. "Mughadara jamaiya li-qiyadiyin fi sahwat Abu Ghurayy-ib ithr sahb silah himayathim wa-tahdidat Al-Qaida" ("The Mass Departure of Commanders from the Abu Ghraib Sahwa in the Wake of the Withdrawal of Their Bodyguards' Weapons and the Threats from Al-Qaida"), *Al-Sumarriya News* (Baghdad), November 22, 2010, available from *www.sumarianews.com/ar/13898/print-article.htm*.

58. Timothy Williams and Duraid Adnan, "Sunnis in Iraq Allied with U.S. Quitting to Rejoin Rebels," *The New York Times*, October 16, 2010, available from *www.nytimes.com*.

59. Information from the author's wife, who served as an interpreter with the U.S. Army in Iraq, 2008-10.

60. Muhammad Hamid Al-Sawwaf, "Sunnat Al-Iraq wa-tumuh al-awda ila al-sulta; Al-Qawa'im al-alamaniya taktasih Al-Mawsil wa-Salah Al-Din wa'l-Anbar" ("Iraq's Sunnis and Their Desire to Return to Power; The Secular Parties Sweep Mosul, Salah Al-Din, and Al-Anbar"), Shabakat Al-Naba' Al-Malumatiya (Baghdad), March 10, 2010, available from *www.annabaa.org/nbanews/2010/03/134.htm*.

61. Tim Arango and Kareem Fahim, "Iraq Again Uses Sunni Tribesmen in Militant War," *The New York Times*, January 19, 2014,

available from *www.nytimes.com*; Jane Arraf, "Iraq's Sunni Tribal Leaders Say Fight for Fallujah Is Part of a Revolution," *The Washington Post*, March 12, 2014, available from *www.washingtonpost. com*; and "Al-Jaysh al-iraqi maduman bi'l-asha'ir yakhud maarik ma DAISH fi Al-Ramadi" ("The Iraqi Army Supported by the Tribes Enters into Battle against the Islamic State in Iraq and Syria in Ramadi"), *Al-Sharq Al-Awsat*, January 20, 2014, available from *www.aawsat.com/print.asp?did=758264&issueno=12837.*

62. "Na'ib an Dawlat Al-Qanun yattahim sahwat Babil bi'l-taharrub min ada' wajibhim" ("A Parliamentarian Belonging to [Maliki's] State of Law Coalition Accuses the Babil Sahwa of Shirking Its Duty"), Al-Sumarriya TV, January 18, 2014, available from *www.alsumaria.tv/news/90937.*

63. "Musallahu asha'ir arabiya yuhajimun Al-Bashmarga ma tajaddud al-ishtibakat ma DAISH fi Al-Jawla'" ("Fighters from Arab Tribes Attack the Peshmerga While Clashes against ISIS Break Out Again in Al-Jawla'"), *Shafaq News*, June 13, 2014, available from *www.shafaaq.com.*

64. "Sa-nastain bihim," and "Sulfa bi-mablagh 150 milyar dinar rawatib al-sahwat" ("Loan of 150 b Dinars for the Sahwa Salaries"), Al-Sumarriya TV, June 21, 2013, available from *www. alsumaria.tv/news/78131.*

65. "Al-Hukuma al-iraqiya tuhyi al-sahwat" ("The Iraqi Government Revives the Sahwa"), Al-Jazira TV, August 25, 2013, available from *www.aljazeera.net;* and "Taayyan 16 alf unsur jadid fi al-sahwat" ("16,000 New Members Inducted in the Sahwa"), Shabakat Al-Ilam Al-Iraqi (Baghdad), December 10, 2013, available from *www.imn.iq/news/view.32636.*

66. "Al-Hukuma al-iraqiya tuhyi al-sahwat" ("The Iraqi Government Revives the Sahwa"), Al-Jazira TV, August 25, 2013, available from *www.aljazeera.net;* "Taayyan 16 alf unsur," and "Al-Quwwat al-barriya tabda' bi-taslih al-sahwat fi Karkuk wa-majlis Al-Hawija yutalib al-difa bi-tayin 600 unsur" ("The Army Begins to Arm the Sahwa in Kirkuk and the Al-Hawija Council Requests from the Ministry of Defense the Hiring of 600 Personnel"), Al-Sumarriya TV, January 19, 2014, available from *www. alsumaria.tv/news/91013.*

67. "Sahwat Al-Iraq: Shuyukh asha'ir mana bi'l-nahar wa-diddana bi'l-layl" ("The Sahwa of Iraq: Tribal Shaykhs Are with Us during the Day and against Us at Night"), *Al-Jiwar*, January 13, 2014, available from *www.aljewar.org/print-48093.aspx*.

68. "Sahwat Diyala tujaddid mutalabatha bi-tashkil liwa'iha al-khass wa-tuhadhdhir min tanami qudrat Al-Qaida" ("The Diyala Sahwa Renews Its Request for the Creation of Its Own Brigade and Warns of Al-Qaida's Improved Capabilities"), Al-Sumarriya TV, October 7, 2013, available from *www.alsumaria.tv/news/84024*.

69. "*Al-Sabah Al-Jadid* tanshur bunud mubadarat Al-Anbar" ("*Al-Sabah Al-Jadid* Publishes the Terms of the Al-Anbar Initiative"), *Al-Sabah Al-Jadid*, February 7, 2014, available from *www.newsabah.com*; and "Harb Al-Anbar kallafat al-dawla 20 milyar dular" ("The Anbar War Costs the State $20 Billion"), *Babil* (Baghdad), May 4, 2014, available from *www.babil.info/printVersion.php?mid=44574*.

70. "Masadir mawsiliya: Iltihaq quwwat min al-jaysh wa'l-shurta bi-DAISH bi-sabab tasarrufat Swat" ("Mosul Sources: Army and Police Personnel Go Over to ISIS because of the Swat Force's Actions"), Ur News Agency (Baghdad), June 11, 2014, available from *www.uragency.net*; and Wa'il Nima, "Al-Anbar takhsha 'harb tha'rat' wa-rijalha mustaiddun li-tard DAISH idha taghayyar ra'is al-hukuma" ("Al-Anbar Fears a 'War of Revenge' and Its Men Are Prepared to Expel ISIS If the Prime Minister Is Changed"), *Al-Mada*, June 4, 2014, available from *almadapaper.net/ar/printnews.aspx?NewsID=465766*. (Hereafter Nima, "Al-Anbar takhsha.")

71. Ahmad Abu Risha quoted in "Abu Risha: 40 bi'l-mi'a min Al-Anbar bi-yad Al-Qaida bi-sabab ida'iyat al-jaysh li-ahali al-muhafazha" ("Abu Risha: 40 Percent of Al-Anbar Is in Al-Qaida's Hands Due to the Army's Hostility to the Province's Population"), *Al-Mustaqbal* (Baghdad), October 25, 2013, available from *almustaqbalnews.net/news/world/item/22289*; and "Al-Anbar: al-sahwat milishiyat wa-alayna inha' tawajudha fi al-muhafazha" ("Al-Anbar: The Sahwa Is a Militia and We Must Eliminate It in the Province"), *Al-Madar* (Baghdad), November 12, 2013, available from *www.almadarnews.info/index.php?page=article&id=3302*.

72. Wad Al-Shammari, "Masadir: 1850 qatilan wa-5 alaf ja-rih khasa'ir al-jaysh fi Al-Anbar wa'l-amaliyat tafqud 128 ajalat Hummer wa-7 mudarraat wa-dabbabtayn" ("Sources: 1850 Killed and 5000 Wounded in Al-Anbar and the Operational Force Loses 128 Humvees, 7 Armored Vehicles, and 2 Tanks"), *Al-Sabah Al-Jadid*, May 11, 2014, available from *www.newsabah.com*.

73. Mustafa Nasir and Haytham Nazhar, "Al-Amn wa'l-difa al-barlamaniya fi hira min wad al-jaysh fi Al-Anbar" ("Parliament's Security and Defense Committee at a Loss over the Army's Situation in Al-Anbar"), *Al-Alam*, (Baghdad), May 15, 2014, available from *www.alaalem.com/index.php?aa=news&id22=15870*.

74. Mustafa Muhammad, "Khabir askari: Adam al-mihni-ya wa-taati al-mukhaddirat wara' taraju al-mu'assasa al-alas-kariya" ("A Defense Expert: A Lack of Professionalism and Drug Use Are behind the Military Establishment's Retreat"), *Al-Alam*, June 12, 2014, available from *www.alaalem.com/index.php?aa=news&id22=18182*; "Na'ib kurdistani: Qada askariyin (sic) taraku aslihathum wa-laja'u ila al-iqlim" ("A Kurdish Member of Parliament: Military Commanders Abandoned Their Weapons and Have Taken Refuge in Our Canton"), Ur News Agency, June 10, 2014, available from *www.uragency.net*; and "Mas'ulun: DAISH ikhtaraqat 3 alwiya wa-fatahat satiran turabiyan yuhit bi-Samarra'" ("Officials: ISIS Overran 3 Brigades and Penetrated the Earth Berm Surrounding Samarra"), *Al-Madar*, June 7, 2014, available from *www.almadarnews.info/index.php?page=article&id=4530*.

75. Walid Mahdi, "Masdar askari yakshif asbab fashl tahrir Al-Falluja" ("A Military Source Reveals the Reasons for the Failure to Liberate Falluja"), Ur News Agency, May 13, 2014, available from *www.uragency.net*.

76. "DAISH yuhdhir al-mutahalifin mau man 'shaqq asa al-jamaa' wa-yatawaad bi-hadm al-mazarat" ("ISIS Cautions Its Allies against 'Deviating from the Rest' and Promises to Demolish the Shrines"), *Shafaq News* (Baghdad), June 13, 2014, available from *www.shafaaq.com*; and Patrick Cockburn, "Iraq Crisis: As the Sunni Terror Spreads, Its Fighters Look for Wives," *The Independent* (London), June 22, 2014, available from *www.independent.co.uk*.

77. Nima, "Al-Anbar takhsha," "Rijal al-din bi-Naynawa yunaddidun bi-DAISH wa'l-jaysh yastaidd li-taslih al-asha'ir al-mahalliya" ("The Clerics in Naynawa Condemn ISIS and the Army Is Preparing to Arm the Local Tribes"), *Mawtini* (Baghdad), June 12, 2014, available from *mawtani.al-shorfa.com/ar/articles/iii/ features/2014/06/12/feature01.*

78. "Iltihaq 300 shabb falluji bi-fawj al-asha'ir li-muharabat DAISH" ("300 Youths from Falluja Join the Tribal Force to Fight ISIS"), *Al-Jiwar*, May 20, 2014, available from *www.aljewar.org/ print-49537.aspx;* and "Asha'ir Naynawa taqtul 23 daishiyan bi'l-Mawsil wa-tabda' bi-tahrir Hayy Al-Wahda" ("The Naynawa Tribes Kill 23 from ISIS and Begin the Liberation of Mosul's Al-Wahda Neighborhood"), *Al-Jiwar*, June 12, 2014, available from *www.aljewar.org/news-49719.aspx.*

79. "Sahwat Diyala tu'akkid istidadha li-muwajahat DAISH wa-tutalib bi-taslihha wa-damha" ("The Diyala Sahwa Reasserts Its Readiness to Confront ISIS and Requests Arms and Support"), *Shafaq News*, June 10, 2014, available from *www.shafaaq. com;* "Quwwat al-asha'ir tusaytir ala Al-Duluiya wa-tataqil 7 min DAISH bad ishtibakat anifa" ("Tribal Forces Take Control of Al-Duluiya and Capture 7 from ISIS after Violent Clashes"), *Shafaq News*, June 14, 2014, available from *www.shafaaq.com;* and Muhammad Sabah, "Al-Anbar: Al-Qa'im tuqawim wa-mas'uluha yatlubun tazizat askariya ajila" ("Al-Anbar: Al-Qa'im Resists and Its Officials Request Urgent Military Reinforcements"), *Al-Mada*, June 20, 2014, available from *alamadapaper.net/ar/printnews. aspx?NewsID=466767.*

80. "Mutatawwiu Al-Anbar: Nahtaj li-asliha wa-isnad min al-jaysh wa-Haditha ma zal tuqawim" ("The Al-Anbar Volunteers: We Need Weapons and Support from the Army and Haditha Is Still Resisting"), *Al-Alam*, June 24, 2014, available from *www. alaalem.com.*

81. "Asha'ir Al-Furat Al-Awsat talabba dawat al-marjaiya bi-istirad jamahiri yantahi ind maktab al-imam Al-Sistani" ("The Tribes of the Central Euphrates Respond to the Call from the Religious Leadership for a Mass Parade That Will Culminate at the Office of Imam Al-Sistani"), *Al-Furat News* (Iraq), June 16, 2014, available from *www.alforatnews.com/modules/news/print.*

php?storyid=56895; "Asha'ir Kab fi Al-Basra tulin tatawwuha li'l-difa an al-watan wa'l-muqaddasat" ("The Kab Tribes in Basra Declare They Are Volunteering to Defend the Nation and the Holy Places"), *Al-Sabah Al-Jadid*, June 17, 2014, available from *www.newsabah.com/wp/newspaper/9017*; and "Indammat quwwat majalis al-isnad wa'l-sahwat ila al-mutatawwiin li-muharabat DAISH al-irhabi talbiyatan li-dawat al-marjaiya al-diniyaal-ulya wa-ulama' al-muslimin min jami al-tawa'if" ("The Forces of the Support Councils and the Sahwa Join the Volunteers to Fight the Terrorist ISIS in Response to the Call by the Supreme Religious Authority and the Muslim Ulama' of All Sects"), *Al-Sabah*, June 17, 2014, available from *www.alsabaah.iq/ArticlePrint.aspx?ID=72941*.

82. "Tazhahura fi Al-Najaf ta'yidan li-fatwa al-marjaiya" ("A Rally in Najaf in Support of the Religious Authority's Fatwa"), *Al-Sabah*, June 16, 2014, available from *www.alsabaah.iq/ArticlePrint.aspx?ID=72861*.

83. "Mutalabat siyasiya fi Al-Basra bi-taskil wizara askariya radifa li-wizarat al-difa" ("Demands in Basra for the Creation of a Reserve Military Ministry in Addition to the Ministry of Defense"), Al-Sumarriya TV, June 14, 2014, available from *www.alsumaria.tv/news/103162*.

84. "Dawawinha tatahawwal ila marakiz tatawwu ma ilan al-bara'a min al-muntamin li'l-tanzhim al-irhabi" ("Its Council Houses Are Transformed into Volunteer Centers after the Proclamation of Shunning Anyone Who Belongs to the Terrorist Organization"), *Al-Sabah*, June 24, 2014, available from *www.alsabaah.iq/ArticleShow.aspx?ID=73389*.

85. Liz Sly, "Maliki Tightens His Grip on Power," *The Washington Post*, June 18, 2014, pp. A1, A4.

86. Ghaith Abdul-Ahad, "Al-Qaida's Wretched Utopia and the Battle for Hearts and Minds," *The Guardian* (London), April 30, 2012, available from *www.guardian.co.uk*.

87. "Maqtal 4 askariyin wa-13 musallah min Al-Qaida fi Al-Yaman wa-Zunjubar 'madinat ashbah'" ("Four Soldiers and Thirteen Al-Qaida Armed Elements Killed in Yemen and Zunjubar Is a "Ghost Town"), *Al-Sharq Al-Awsat*, June 20, 2011, available from *www.aawsat.com/print.asp?did=627347&issueno=11892*.

88. "Ansar Al-Sharia yulinun an istratijiya jadida wa-taktikat mukhtalifa li-harb mudun wasafuha bi'l-anifa" ("The Ansar Al-Sharia Announce a New Strategy and Different Tactics for Urban Operations, Which They Describe As Violent"), *Taqrir Ikhbari*, Madad Al-Ikhbariya, No. 1, September 2011, p. 1.

89. Arafat Madabish, "Milishiyat Al-Yaman . . . Algham al-mustaqbal" ("Yemen's Militias . . . Future Landmines"), *Al-Sharq Al-Awsat*, July 13, 2012, available from *www.aawsat.com/print. asp?did=686108&issueno=12281*.

90. Hamza Al-Zunjubari, "Hamza Al-Zunjubari: Ali Muhsin talab min al-wusata' iblagh al-asra an dughutu kanat wara' iltlaqhim!" ("Hamza Al-Zunjubari: Ali Muhsin Asked the Mediators to Inform the Prisoners That It Was His Pressure That Was Behind Their Release"), *Taqrir Ikhbari*, Madad Al-Ikhbariya, No. 18, May 2012, p. 4; and "Al-Amrikiyun yulhibun sama' Al-Yaman" ("The Americans Set Yemen's Skies Ablaze"), *Taqrir Ikhbari*, Madad Al-Ikhbariya, No. 19, May 2012, p. 1.

91. "Bad muhawalat ightiyal shakhsiya qabaliya tawattur shadid bayn Al-Qaida wa'l-qaba'il fi Abyan" ("Following an Attempt to Assassinate a Tribal Notable Serious Tension between Al-Qaida and the Tribes"), *Akhbar Aden*, December 2, 2011, available from *www.aden-news.net/nprint.php?lng=arabic&sid=8355*.

92. "Al-Liqa' al-maftuh ma al-mas'ul al-shari li-tanzhim Qaidat Jazirat Al-Arab" ("The Open Interview with the Legal Representative of Al-Qaida in the Arabian Peninsula"), n.d. (2011), available from *www.as-ansar.com/vb/showthread.php?t=37181*.

93. "Al Qaeada Militants Take Control of Another Yemen Province," *The National* (Dubai, UAE), March 12, 2012, available from *www.thenational.ae/news/world/al-qaead-militants-take-control-of-another-yemen-province*.

94. "Asharat min anasir Al-Qaida yatamarkazun fi mint-aqat Al-Udayn bi-madinat Ibb" ("Dozens of Al-Qaida Members Congregate in the Al-Udayn Section of the City of Ibb"), *Al-Wasat* (Baghdad), March 31, 2013, available from *www.alwasat-ye. net/?ac=3&no=35656&d_f=38&t_f=0&t=5&lanf_in*.

95. "Iqamat al-hudud al-shariya fi madinat Jaar" ("Imple-menting the Legal Penalties in the City of Jaar"), *Taqrir Ikhbari, Madad Al-Ikhbariya,* No. 2, October 2011, p. 2; and "Ansar al-Sharia yaqbidun ala sahir fi Jaar" ("The Ansar Al-Sharia Arrest a Sorcerer in Jaar"), *Taqrir Ikhbari,* Madad Al-Ikhbariya, No. 3, October 2011, p. 2.

96. "Ansar Al-Sharia yaqbidun ala sahir fi Jaar" ("The Ansar Al-Sharia Arrest a Sorcerer in Jaar"), p. 2; "Tahdhir hamm li'l-sa-hara" ("An Important Warning to Sorcerers"), *Akhbar Al-Saa* (Sa-naa), August 6, 2013, available from *hournews.net/news-21347.htm;* "Al-Qaida tuhaddid al-mashudhin bi-Hadramwat bi'l-tasfiya wa-mashudh yulin tawbathu bad istihdaf sahir" ("Al-Qaida Threat-ens Deviants with Death and a Deviant Repents After a Sorcerer Is Targeted"), *Al-Mashhad Al-Yamani* (Sanaa), August 5, 2013, avail-able from *almashad-alyemeni.com/news30788.html;* Amal Al-Yarisi, "Folk Superstitions in Yemen: Bad Luck Or Good Luck?" *Yemen Times* (Sanaa), June 3, 2013, available from *www.yementimes.com;* and Dr. Zaynab, "Man wara' intishar al-sihr wa'l-shuudha fi Al-Yaman?" ("Who Is Behind the Spread of Sorcery and Deviance in Yemen?"), *Akhbar Al-Yawm* (Sanaa), June 29, 2010, available from *www.akhbaralyom.net/articles.php?id=61973.*

97. "Ansar Al-Sharia fi Rida yu'akkidun ann al-nizham al-fasid al-zhalim la yanfa mah illa al-jihad li-radih wa-radd zhul-mih" ("The Ansar Al-Sharia in Rida Confirm That the Only Way to Deal with the Corrupt and Unjust Regime Is by the Jihad in Order to Foil It and Resist Its Injustice"), *Taqrir Ikhbari,* Madad Al-Ikhbariya, No. 9, February 2012, p. 1.

98. Arafat Madabish, "Qaba'il Abyan tantafid didd Al-Qaida wa-qatla bi'l-asharat fi sufuf al-musallahin" ("The Tribes of Abyan Revolt against Al-Qaida and There Are Dead by the Dozens in the Ranks of the Combatants"), *Al-Sharq Al-Awsat,* July 19, 2012, avail-able from *www.aawsat.com/print.asp?did=631737&issueno=11921.*

99. Jalal Al-Marqashi, Interview with Abd Al-Razzaq Al-Ja-mal, *Al-Quds Al-Arabi* (London), May 5, 2012, available from *www.alquds.co.uk/index.asp?fname=data/2012/05/05-13/13qpt962.htm.*

100. "Shahid bi'l-vidiyu: Anasir Al-Qaida yudimun muwatin bi-madinat Jaar janub Al-Yaman" ("See the Video: Al-Qaida Elements Execute a Citizen in the City of Jaar in South Yemen"), *Aden Al-Ghad* (Aden), September 30, 2011, available from *adenalghad. net/printpost/3978*.

101. Sudarsan Raghavan, "In Yemen, Tribal Militias in a Fierce Battle with Al-Qaeda Wing," *The Washington Post*, September 10, 2012, available from *www.washingtonpost.com*.

102. Abd Al-Razzaq Al-Jamal, "Mustaqbal muhafazhat Ibb bad inhiyar al-ittifaq bayn al-amn al-siyasi wa-a'idi Ansar Al-Sharia" ("The Future of Ibb Province Following the Collapse of the Agreement Between the Political Security and the Ansar Al-Sharia Returning from Abyan"), Al-Majlis Al-Yamani forum (Sanaa), December 6, 2013, available from *www.yemen-forum.net/vb/ showthread.php?t=701364*.

103. Interview with Maddah Muhammad Awad, "Kayf zhaharat al-lijan al-shabiya fi Lawdar?" *Aden Al-Ghad*, March 9, 2013, available from *adenalghad.net/news/41870*.

104. "Qissat al-musallahin fi Abyan" ("Account of the Armed Elements in Abyan"), *Al-Ghad* (Sanaa), Part 2, August 24, 2011, available from *www.aghadayem.net/print.php?id=5450*.

105. *Ibid.*; and "Ihtijajan ala taslim mustahaqqathim ila ahad al-masha'ikh al-lijan al-shabiya tunazhzhim waqfa ihtijajiya amam manzil muhafizh Abyan wa-tuhaddid al-tasid" ("Complaining That Their Salaries Are Disbursed Through a Tribal Leader, the Popular Committees Stage a Protest in Front of the Governor of Abyan's Residence and Threaten to Escalate"), *Akhbar Al-Yawm*, December 30, 2012, available from *www.akhbaralyom.net/nprint. php?lng=arabic&sid=63050*.

106. "Fi-ma tazhahurat ihtijajiyat li'l-lijan al-shabiya bi-ahwar li'l-mutalaba bi-huquqhim" ("Protests by the Popular Committees in Ahwar Demanding Their Rights"), *Akhbar Al-Yawm*, January 20, 2013, available from *www.akhbaralyom.net/ print.php?lng=arabic&sid=63741*; and "Fi ijtima damm mudara' al-mudiriyat wa-qiyadat al-lijan al-shabiya bi-Lahij Al-Majidi yu'akkid tashkil al-lijan min al-atilin wa'l-Sabihi yuhadhdhir min

dukhul anasir qaidiya wa-huthiya" ("In a Meeting That Brought Together District Governors and Popular Committee Leaders in Lahij, Al-Majidi Confirms the Formation of Committees from the Unemployed and Al-Sabihi Warns about Al-Qaida and Houthi Elements Joining"), *Akhbar Al-Yawm*, October 23, 2012, available from *akhbaralyom.net/nprint.php?lng=arabic&sid=60616*; and "Zunjubar: Insihab Al-Qaida wa'l-dawla aydan" ("Zunjubar: The Retreat of Al-Qaida and Also of Its State"), *Aden Al-Ghad*, July 13, 2013, available from *adenalghad.net/printpost/57519*.

107. "Al-Lijan al-shabiya fi Abyan tudim jundi bi-tuhmat shrub al-khamr" ("The Popular Committees Execute a Soldier for the Crime of Drinking Alcohol"), *Bawwabat Al-Yaman* (Yemen), June 24, 2013, available from *gateyemen.com/ar/news11805.html*; and Samir Hasan, "Ittihamat bi-iadamat maydaniya fi Al-Yaman" ("Accusations of Summary Executions in Yemen"), Al-Jazira TV, August 11, 2012, available from *www.aljazeera.net*.

108. Interview with Abd Al-Latif Al-Sayyid, "Muhafazhat al-ra'is fi qabdat al-lijan al-shabiya" ("The President's Home Province Is in the Grip of the Popular Committees"), *Al-Masdar* (Sanaa), January 21, 2013, available from *almasdaronline.com/article/print/40671*.

109. "Al-Lijan al-shabiya takshir an anyabha wa-tawattur fi Zunjubar wa-Shaqra wa-Lawdar" ("The Popular Committees Bare Their Teeth and Tension in Zunjubar, Shaqra, and Lawdar"), *Radfan Press* (Yemen), July 29, 2012, available from *www.rdfanpress.net/nprint.php?lng=arabic&sid=5195*; and Abd Al-Ilah Sumayh. "Abyan: Nahb manazil al-nazihin tatasabbab bi-tabadul al-ittihamat bayn al-lijan al-shabiya wa'l=jaysh" ("Abyan: The Looting of Refugees' Houses Leads to Mutual Accusations between the Popular Committees and the Army"), *Aden On Line*, June 22, 2012, available from *www.aden-online.com/news/108201*.

110. "Fi arqala wadiha li-iltizamat al-hukuma tujah al-manihin wa-asdiqa' Al-Yaman" ("A Clear Obstruction to the Government's Obligations to Its Donors and the Friends of Yemen"), *Akhbar Al-Yawm*, May 15, 2014, available from *www.akhbaralyom.net/nprint.php?lng=arabic&sid=79307*; and "Itiqal qurabat 45 min afrad al-liwa' 111 bi-Abyan baynhum 4 dubbat mutawarritin bi'l-tawatu' ma Al-Qaida" ("The Arrest of Some 45 Personnel from

the 111th Brigade in Abyan Including 4 Officers Involved in Colluding with Al-Qaida"), *Yemen Press* (Sanaa), December 7, 2013, available from *yemen-press.com/news25139.html*.

111. "Wisata qabaliya tafshal bi-ibqa' al-jaysh fi Al-Mahfad" ("Tribal Intercession Fails to Keep the Army in Al-Mahfad"), *Al-Yaman Al-Yawm* (Sanaa), November 2013, available from *www.yemen-today.net/DetailsNews.aspx?ID=98*.

112. For an excellent overview of the 2012 military campaign, see W. Andrew Terrill, *The Struggle for Yemen and the Challenge of Al-Qaeda in the Arabian Peninsula*, Carlisle, PA: Strategic Studies Institute, U.S. Army War College, June 2013.

113. Sam Kimball, "Yemenis Left with Mixed Feelings after Government Troops Oust Islamists," *The Guardian*, July 20, 2012, available from *www.guardian.co.uk/world/2012/jul/20/yemen-islamist-al-qaida-abyan/print*.

114. "Al-Lijan al-shabiya fi Abyan tajriba najiha" ("The Popular Committees in Abyan Are a Success"), *14 Uktubir* (Aden), January 12, 2014, available from *www.14october.com/news.aspx?newsno=3063606*.

115. "Al-Jaysh yusaytir ala Azzan ithr ishtibakat ma al-lijan al-shabiya asfarat an 4 jarha" ("The Army Takes Over in Azzan Following Clashes with the Popular Committees That Resulted in Four Wounded"), *Akhbar Al-Yawm*, July 5, 2012, available from *www.akhbaralyom.net/nprint.php?lng=arabic&sid=56262*.

116. "Lawdar: Qissat am li'l-madina allati hazamat Al-Qaida" ("Lawdar: Story of a Year of the City That Defeated Al-Qaida"), *Aden Al-Ghad*, April 9, 2013, available from *adenalghad.net/printpost/45926*; and "Tarhil anasir min Al-Qaida ila madinat Adan yuthir ghadab al-ahali bi-Lawdar" ("The Transfer of Al-Qaida Personnel to Aden Angers the Citizens of Lawdar"), *Aden Al-Ghad*, April 18, 2013, available from *adenalghad.net/printpost/47070*.

117. "Maqtal 230 jundiyan yamaniyan bi-Zunjubar" ("230 Yemeni Soldiers Dead in Zunjubar"), Al-Jazira TV, September 11, 2011, available from *www.aljazeera.net*.

118. "Mas'ul amni yamani li'l-*Sharq*: Al-Qaida taghtal 10 ju-nud muqabil maqtal ayy unsur minha bi'l-ta'irat al-amrikiya" ("A Yemeni Security Official Tells *Al-Sharq*: Al-Qaida Kills 10 Soldiers for Every One of Its Members That American Aircraft Kill), *Al-Sharq* (Najran, Saudi Arabia"), February 4, 2013.

119. "Al-Lijan al-shabiya bi-Zunjubar tanshar tamiman bi-man harakat al-darajat al-nariya bad al-saa al-tasia masa'an wa-man anashid Al-Qaida" ("The Popular Committees in Zun-jubar Emit a Circular Forbidding Motorcycle Traffic after Nine O'Clock in the Evening and Al-Qaida Slogans"), *Al-Hadrami Al-Yawm*,(Yemen), April 19, 2014.

120. "Al-Lijan al-shabiya fi Abyan."

121. "Al-Habba al-shabiya addat ila imhisar dawr tanzhim Al-Qaida fi Hadramawt" ("The Popular Movement Has Led to a Retrenchment in Al-Qaida's Activity"), *Yafa News* (Yemen), De-cember 26, 2013, available from *www.yafa-news.net/archives/83938*.

122. "Dabt ahad al-anasir al-irhabiya wa-huwa yartadi hizam nasif fi urs bi-Abyan" ("The Arrest of a Terrorist Operative Wear-ing an Explosive Vest at a Wedding in Abyan"), Yemen Ministry of the Interior website, January 5, 2014.

123. "Fi arqala wadiha," and Interview by Isam Ali Muham-mad with Abd Al-Latif Al-Sayyid, "Yatahaddath Abd Al-Latif Al-Sayyid qa'id al-lijan al-shabiya fi Abyan li-*Akhbar Al-Yawm*" ("Abd Al-Latif Al-Sayyid, commander of the Popular Commit-tees in Abyan Talks with *Akhbar Al-Yawm*"), *Akhbar Al-Yawm*, November 30, 2013, available from *www.akhbaralyom.net/nprint. php?lng=arabic&sid=6916*.

124. "Akkad annahum yaqumun bi-dawr al-shurta fi al-ma-dina" ("He Stressed That They Were Acting As the Police in the City"), *Aden Al-Ghad*, April 22, 2014, available from *adenalghad. net/news/102111*.

125. "Hamla askariya bi-musharakat al-lijan al-shabiya bi-Ahwar li-taaqqub anasir Al-Qaida" ("A Military Campaign with the Participation of the Popular Committees in Ahwar in Pursuit of the Al-Qaida Elements"), *Aden Al-Ghad*, April 29, 2014, avail-able from *adenalghad.net/news/103152*.

126. "Al-Ra'is wa'l-dakhiliya yatarifan bi-tazayud khatar Al-Qaida" ("The President and the Ministry of the Interior Admit to a Rising Threat from Al-Qaida"), *Al-Wasat*, May 21, 2014, available from *alwasat-ye.net/index.php?ac=3&no=39142&d_f=15&t_f=0&t=5&lang_in=Ar*.

127. "Al-Jaysh al-yamani yuqhim lijan Abyan al-shabiya fi khatt al-muwajaha ma tanzhim Al-Qaida al-yawm al-thalatha'" ("Last Tuesday the Yemeni Army Throws the Abyan Tribal Committee into the Front Lines of a Fight against Al-Qaida"), *Al-Hadrami Al-Yawm*, April 29, 2014, available from *alhadramyalyoum.blogspot.com/2014/04/blog-post_2353.html*.

128. "Al-Qabd ala irhabi hawal al-tasallul ila ihda thuknat al-junud fi Shabwa" ("Seizure of a Terrorist Who Tried to Penetrate One of the Military Barracks"), Yemeni Ministry of the Interior website, May 8, 2014, available from *www.smc.gov.ye*; and "Al-Uthur ala asliha wa-mutafajjirat fi manzil ahad ada' Al-Qaida bi-Abyan" ("The Discovery of Arms and Explosives in the House of an Al-Qaida Member in Abyan"), *14 Uktubir*, May 8, 2014, available from *www.14october.com/news.aspx?newsno=3070873*.

129. Ali Mansur Miqrat, "Qiyadat al-lijan al-shabiya tu'akkid al-qital ma al-jaysh li-tathir Al-Mahfad min al-irhabiyin" ("The Popular Committee Commanders Confirm They Are Fighting Alongside the Army to Clear Terrorists from Al-Mahfad"), *14 Uktubir*, May 4, 2014, available from *www.14october.com/news.aspx?newsno=3070590*.

130. "Amrika al-salibiya tasa li-ihkam ihtilal Jazirat Al-Arab intilaqan min Al-Yaman" ("Crusader America Seeks to Consolidate Its Occupation of the Arabian Peninsula Starting from Yemen"), *Taqrir Ikhbari*, Madad Al-Ikhbariya, No. 26, November 2012, p. 4.

131. "Bayan li-Ansar Al-Sharia bi-khusus al-lijan al-shabiya fi Abyan" ("Communique from the Ansar Al-Sharia on the Subject of the Popular Committees in Abyan"), reproduced in *Akhbar Al-Saa*, April 19, 2014, available from *hournews.net/print.php?id=29132*.

132. "Ra'is majlis qaba'il Bakil li'l-silm wa'l-islah al-shaykh Afraj: Qaba'il al-Yaman tarfud an tatahawwal ila adat fi al-harb ala Al-Qaida" ("Shaykh Afraj, the Head of the Bakil Tribal Con-federation Council, Who Supports Peace and Reform: Yemen's Tribes Refuse to Become a Tool in the War against Al-Qaida"), *Al-Wasat* (Manama, Bahrain), January 9, 2010, available from *www.alwasatnews.com/2692/news/read/362750/1.html*.

133. *Ibid.*

134. Samir Hasan, "Al-Lijan al-shabiya tuthir qalaqan Janub Al-Yaman" ("The Popular Committees Give Rise to Concern in Southern Yemen"), Al-Jazira TV, July 7, 2012, available from *www.aljazeera.net*.

135. Arafat Madabish, "Al-Yaman: Tahrir imarat Azzan min Al-Qaida" ("Yemen: The Liberation of the Emirate of Azzan from Al-Qaida"), *Al-Sharq Al-Awsat*, June 24, 2012, available from *www.aawsat.com/print.asp?did=683253&issueno=12262*.

136. *Ibid.*; and Samir Hasan, "Makhawif min awdat Al-Qaida ila Abyan" ("Fears of Al-Qaida's Return to Abyan"), Al-Jazira TV, August 1, 2012, available from *www.aljazerra.net*.

137. "Najat qa'id al-lijan al-shabiya min muhawalat ightiyal wa-isabat jundiyayn bi-rasas Al-Qaida" ("Popular Committee Commander Survives an Assassination Attempt and Two Sol-diers Are Hit by Al-Qaida Bullets"), *Shabwa Press* (Ataq, Yemen), September 12, 2013, available from *shabwaahpress.net/news/9531*.

138. Raghavan.

139. "Al-Lijan al-shabiya bi-Mukayras tunashid wazir al-difa bi-iqaf mustahaqqat al-lijan al-wahmiya" ("The Popular Commit-tees in Mukayras Petition the Minister of Defense to Stop the Sala-ries of the Fictional Committees"), *Aden Al-Ghad*, August 6, 2013, available from *adenalghad.net/news/60418*.

140. "Akkad annahum yaqumun bi-dawr al-shurta fi al-ma-dina" ("He Stressed That They Were Acting As the Police in the City"), *Aden Al-Ghad*, April 22, 2014, available from *adenalghad.net/news/102111*.

141. Muhammad Al-Abasi, "Bi'l-Watha'iq fasad wizarat al-difa al-yamaniya yaltahim mukhassasat al-lijan al-shabiya fi Abyan" ("Documentary Proof of Corruption in Yemen's Ministry of Defense Gobbling Up the Allocations for the Popular Committees in Abyan"), *Sabq News* (Yemen), March 7, 2013.

142. "Afrad min al-lijan al-shabiya fi manatiq bi-Tibn Lahij yarfaun shakwa li-wazir al-difa" ("Members of the Popular Committees in the Tibn Lahij Area Complain to the Minister of Defense"), *Aden Al-Ghad*, December 19, 2013, available from *aden-alghad.net/news/82815*; and "Ada' fi al-lijan al-shabiya bi-Lawdar yashkun adam sarf murattabathim" ("Members of the Popular Committees in Lawdar Complain About Not Receiving Their Salaries"), *Aden Al-Ghad*, April 12, 2013, available from *adenalghad. net/news/46328*.

143. *Ibid.*; and Muhammad Abd Al-Alim, "Na'ib ra'is al-lijan al-shabiya bi-muhafazhat Shabwa: Al-Lijan sa-tuqif amalha li-muddat usbu" ("The Deputy Commander of the Popular Committees in Shabwa Province: The Committees Will Suspend Their Activity for a Week"), *Aden Al-Ghad* , January 14, 2014, available from *adenalghad.net/printpost/86679*.

144. "Abyan: Qiyadat al-lijan al-shabiya tulin ikhla' mas'uliyatha an al-amn bi'l-muhafazha" ("The Popular Committees' Leadership Announces It Will Relinquish Its Security Responsibilities in the Province"), *Akhbar Al-Yawm*, February 16, 2014, available from *www.akhbaralyom.net/news_details. php?lng=arabic&sid=76393*.

145. "Al-Lajna al-ulya li'-lijan al-shabiya fi Ataq tuqarrir taliq amal rijalhafi asimat Shabwa" ("The Governing Committee of the Popular Committees in Ataq Decides to Suspend Operations in the Capital of Shabwa"), *Shabwa Press*, May 9, 2014.

146. "Qabaliyun yamnaun al-hamla al-askariya min dukhul Al-Majala" ("Tribesmen Prevent the Military Force from Entering Al-Majala"), *Akhbar Al-Yawm*, May 1, 2014, available from *www. akhbaralyom.net/nprint.php?lng=arabic&sid=78967*.

147. Safiya Al-Awdhali, "Al-Jaysh yaqtahim Al-Majala wa'l-Mahfad fi Abyan wa-Mayfaa fi Shabwa" ("The Army Enters Al-Majala and Al-Mahfad in Abyan and Al-Mayfaa in Shabwa"), *Al-Yaman Al-Yawm*, May 2, 2014, available from *www.yemen-today. net/DetailsNews.aspx?Id=13196.*

148. "Abyan: Muqatilun min al-lijan al-shabiya yanhabun asliha wa-atad tabia li'l-liwa' al-thani mushat jabali" ("Abyan: Fighters from the Popular Committees Loot Arms and Equipment from the 2nd Mountain Infantry Brigade"), *Hashad* (Yemen), April 25, 2014, available from *www.hshd.net/print17321.html.*

149. "Ada' lijan shabiya bi-Lawdar yaqtuun tariqan yarbut bayn Abyan wa-Shabwa ihtijajan ala adam tawzhifhim" ("Members of the Popular Committees in Lawdar Block the Road Connecting Abyan and Shabwa as a Protest for Not Being Hired"), *Aden Al-Ghad*, December 10, 2013, available from *adenalghad.net/news/81545.*

150. "Hal sa-yaud sinariyu Sada fi abyan wa-Shabwa li-tasfiyat al-lijan al-shabiya?" ("Is the Sada Scenario to Be Repeated in Abyan and Shabwa to Liquidate the Popular Committees?"), *Aden Al-Ghad*, May 7, 2014, available from *adenalghad.net/news/104464.*

151. Samir Hasan, "Al-Lijan al-shabiya tuthir qalaqan Janub Al-Yaman" ("The Popular Committees Give Rise to Concern in Southern Yemen"), Al-Jazira TV, July 7, 2012, available from *www.aljazeera.net.*

152. Madabish, "Qaba'il Abyan."

153. "Shuhud: Hujum li'l-jaysh al-yamani yastahdif nuqta qabaliya bi-Hadramawt" ("Eyewitnesses: A Yemeni Army Attack Targets a Tribal Checkpoint in Hadramawt"), *Aden Al-Ghad*, January 24, 2014, available from *adenalghad.net/printpost/88335.*

154. "Muhafizh Abyan wa-qa'id al-mintaqa al-askariya al-rabia yatafaqqadun al-muqatilin wa'l-mu'assasat al-khadamiya wa-yaltaqun bi'l-muwatinin" ("The Governor of Abyan and the Commander of the Fourth Military District Inspect the Troops and the Service Institutions and Meet with the Population"), Ministry of the Interior website, May 8, 2014, available from *www.smc. gov.ye/index.php?option=com_k2&view=item&id=7786.*

155. "Al-Lijan bi-Abyan tulin ta'yidha li-matalib al-mutadar-rarin wa-tumhil al-ra'is 3 ayyam li-iqalat al-muhafizh" ("The Committees in Abyan Declare Their Support for Those Who Suffered Damage and Give the President a Deadline of 3 Days in Which to Remove the Governor"), *Akhbar Al-Yawm*, June 14, 2014, available from *www.akhbaralyom.net/nprint.php?lng=arabic&sid=80103*.

156. "Afrad min al-lijan al-shabiya bi-Radfan yaqtaun al-khatt al-amm wa-yuqifun harakat al-naqilat" ("Members of the Popular Committees in Radfan Block the Public Highway and Stop the Movement of Oil Tankers"), *Aden Al-Ghad*, June 19, 2014, available from *adenalghad.net/printpost/110232*.

157. Interview with Major General Muhammad Nasr by Yahya Al-Sadmi, "Wazir al-difa al-yamani li'l-*Siyasa*: Amaliyatna kasarat shawkat Al-Qaida" ("Yemen's Minister of Defense to *Al-Siyasa*: Our Operations Have Broken the Back of Al-Qaida"), *Al-Siyasa* (Kuwait), May 4, 2014, available from *al-seyassah.com*.

158. "Mufawadat qabaliya ma al-jaysh al-yamani li-waqf al-amaliyat al-askariya muqabil insihab anasir Al-Qaida min Al-Mahfad" ("Tribal Negotiations with the Yemeni Army to End Military Operations in Exchange for Al-Qaida's Departure from Al-Mahfad"), *Aden Free*, May 6, 2014, available from *www.adenfree.com/50933*.

159. "Ansar Al-Sharia yastakmilun intiqalhum ila Hadramawt fajr al-yawm" ("The Ansar Al-Sharia Complete Their Redeployment to Hadramawt This Morning"), *Shabwa Press*, May 9, 2014, available from *www.shabwaahpress.net/news/16660*; and "Asrar tukshaf li-awwwal marra an muwajhat al-jaysh al-yamani wa'l-Qaida bi-Shabwa wa-Abyan" ("Secrets Revealed for the First Time about the Battles between the Yemeni Army and Al-Qaida in Shabwa and Abyan"), *Yafa News*, May 12, 2014, available from *www.yafa-news.net/archives/101112*.

160. "Al-Sahwa takhsha intiqam."

161. Khulud Al-Amiri, "Humma muharabat Al-Qaida tantaqil ila muhafazhat Karkuk" ("The Focus of the Fight against Al-Qaida Shifts to the Province of Kirkuk"), *Al-Hayat*, June 22, 2007, available from *international.daralhayat.com/print/164706/archive*.

162. One intellectual who was skeptical of the effect of tribalism on the prospects for democracy in Iraq even blamed the United States for having reinvigorated tribalism as part of its counterinsurgency strategy, Hasan Nazhim, "Ijtithath al-asha'iriya" ("Detribalization"), *Al-Alam*, January 24, 2010, available from *www.alaalem.com/index.php?aa=news&id22=1187*. Such feelings were present in Yemen as well, Arif BaMu'min, "Al-Lijan al-shabiya fi Hadramawt bayn al-rafd wa'l-qubul" ("The Popular Committees in Hadramawt: To Refuse Or Accept"), *Hadramawt Al-Yawm* (Yemen), November 14, 2013, available from *hadramout-today.net/45303.html*.

163. Shaykh Daydan Abd Allah quoted in "Qiyadi fi al-sahwa: Al-Jaysh al-amiriki akhla al-saha li'l-Qaida li-ta'khudh tha'rha min al-sahwa" ("A Leader in the Sahwa: The American Army Cleared the Field for Al-Qaida to Take Its Revenge against the Sahwa"), Al-Jewar April 5, 2010, available from *www.aljewar.org/news-23213.aspx*.

164. Arif Abu Hatim, "Al-Lijan al-shabiya . . . qunbula mawquta" ("The Popular Committees . . . A Time-Bomb"), Al-Alhale (Yemen), May 16, 2014, available from *alahale.net/article/16483*.

165. Loveday Morris, "To Retake Cities, Iraq Turns to Sunni Tribes," *The Washington Post*, January 30, 2014, available from *www.washingtonpost.com*.

166. "Fi-ma 50 araba mudarraa tantashir ala al-tariq bayn Aden wa-Abyan wa anasir Al-Qaida tughadir Azzan Shabwa" ("As 50 Armored Vehicles Deploy to the Road between Aden and Abyan, Al-Qaida Abandons Azzan in Shabwa"), *Akhbar Al-Yawm*, April 29, 2014, available from *www.akhbaralyom.net/nprint.php?lng=arabic&sid=78915*; Shuaib Almosawa and Eric Schmitt, "2 Yemenis Shot by Americans Are Linked to Qaeda Cell," *New York Times*, May 10, 2014, available from *www.nytimes.com*; and Mohammed Jamjoon and Barbara Starr, "Official: Extensive U.S. Involvement in Anti-Terror Operations in Yemen," CNN News, April 23, 2014, available from *www.cnn.com/2014/04/22/world/meast/yemen-terror-operation-dna*.

167. White House Press Briefing by Press Secretary Jay Carney, January 8, 2014, available from *www.whitehouse.gov/photos-and-video/video/2014/01/08/press-briefings#transcript*.

168. The White House, Office of the Vice President, "Readout of Vice President Biden's Meeting with Iraqi Council of Representatives Speaker Osama al-Nujaifi," January 22, 2014, available from *www.whitehouse.gov/the-press-office/2014/01/22/readout-vice-president-bidens-meeting-iraqi-council-representatives-spea*.

169. Missy Ryan, "U.S. Special Forces Sent to Train Iraqi Special Forces in Jordan," Reuters, March 7, 2014, available from *www.reuters.com/assets/print?aid=USBREA261O420140307*; Michael R. Gordon and Eric Schmitt, "U.S. Sends Arms to Aid Iraq Fight With Extremists," *New York Times*, December 25, 2013, available from *www.nytimes.com*; Qassim Abdul-zahra and Adam Schreck, "Iraq Turns to Sunni Tribes, But Distrust Remains," *Army Times*, February 13, 2014, available from *www.armytimes.com*; "U.S. Drones to the Rescue in Iraq: Strikes Target Al Qaida Strongholds," *World Tribune* (Springfield, VA), January 19, 2014, available from *www.worldtribune.com*; and Loveday Morris, "Interview with Prime Minister Nouri Al-Maliki: Transcript," *The Washington Post*, January 16, 2014, available from *www.washingtonpost.com*.

170. "Algeria to Train Tribal Militia in Mali," Magharebia (USAFRICOM), March 5, 2011, available from *magharebia.com*; and Ahmeyde Ag Ilkamassene, "Mercenariat: Le Mali veut recruter des Imghads d'Algérie pour combattre le MNLA" ("Mercenaries: Mali Wants to Recruit Some of Algeria's Imghad to Fight against the MNLA"), *Amazigh World*, March 21, 2012, available from *www.amazighworld.org/human_rights/index_show.php?id=2858*.

U.S. ARMY WAR COLLEGE

Major General William E. Rapp
Commandant

*****

STRATEGIC STUDIES INSTITUTE
and
U.S. ARMY WAR COLLEGE PRESS

Director
Professor Douglas C. Lovelace, Jr.

Director of Research
Dr. Steven K. Metz

Author
Dr. Norman Cigar

Editor for Production
Dr. James G. Pierce

Publications Assistant
Ms. Rita A. Rummel

*****

Composition
Mrs. Jennifer E. Nevil